C000292419

AQUARIANS TALK TOO think sex is a sporting eve looking things—whether or ally work. Geminis don't p Virgos overspend on miracle cleaners. Scorpios get bored at parties. So do Capricorns, unless the party advances their career. Leos are oversexed. Pisceans are easy marks. Taureans aren't too fond of reading. Repulsing the advances of an Aries isn't the easiest thing in the world.

Don't you wish you'd known this the last time you

* went to a party?

* bought—or sold—a used car?

* accepted a blind date?

* wondered what your boss really meant when he said that?

SUN SIGN
SUCCESS

a bright, fresh and informative view of what Sun Signs *really* mean.

SUN SIGN SUCCESS

Your Astrological Pathway to Better Living

Joseph Polansky

THE AQUARIAN PRESS
Wellingborough, Northamptonshire

First UK Edition 1987

© Joseph Polansky 1977

2   4   6   8   10   9   7   5   3   1

All rights reserved. No part of this book may be reproduced or utilized in any form or by any means, electronic or mechanical, including photocopying, recording or by any information storage and retrieval system, without permission in writing from the Publisher.

ISBN 0-85030-636-1

The Aquarian Press is part of the Thorsons Publishing Group

Printed and bound in Great Britain

Permissions

Reprinted by permission of Sterling Magazine, Inc.

Chapter 1 which originally appeared in *Your Personal Astrology* (Spring 1975) under the title "Why Astrology Really Works" copyright © 1975 by Sterling Magazine, Inc.

Chapter 3 which originally appeared in *Astrology Guide* (January-February 1976) under the title "An Executive's Tour of the Zodiac" copyright © 1976 by Sterling Magazine, Inc.

Chapter 5 which originally appeared in *Astrology Guide* (June 1975) under the title "Astro-Alert" copyright © 1975 by Sterling Magazine, Inc.

Chapter 9 which originally appeared in *Your Personal Astrology* (Winter 1976) under the title of "Love and Sexual Harmony" copyright © 1976 by Sterling Magazine, Inc.

Chapter 11 which originally appeared in *Your Personal Astrology* (Summer 1976) under the title "Zodiac Plan for a Satisfying Vacation" copyright © 1976 by Sterling Magazine, Inc.

Chapter 12 which originally appeared in *Astrology Guide* (May 1975) under the same title, copyright © 1975 by Sterling Magazine, Inc.

Chapter 14 which originally appeared in *Your Personal Astrology* (Spring 1974) under the same title, copyright © 1974 by Sterling Magazine, Inc.

Chapter 18 which originally appeared in *Astrology Guide* (April 1975) under the title "Lunar Timing—When to go After What you Want" copyright © 1975 by Sterling Magazine, Inc.

Chapter 19 originally appeared in *Your Personal Astrology* (Winter 1974) under the same title, copyright © 1974 by Sterling Magazine, Inc.

Chapter 4 will appear in *Astrology—Your Daily Horoscope* in the March 1977 issue under the title "Making the Most of Your Sign" and is reprinted by permission of CBS Publication.

Reprinted by permission of JBH Publications.

Chapter 6 which originally appeared in *Horoscope Guide* (August 1976) under the title "Star Guide to Better Communications" copyright © 1976 by JBH Publications.

Chapter 10 which originally appeared in *Horoscope Guide* (April 1976) under the same title, copyright © 1976 by JBH Publications.

Reprinted by permission of AJA Publishing.

Chapter 7 which originally appeared in *Future Star Horoscope* (October-November 1976) under the title of "You Are What You Read" copyright © 1976 by AJA Publishing.

Dedication

To my mother Fanny Polansky, who never stopped believing in me, even when I did, and who was always there.

Acknowledgments

Writing a book is always a group effort. Many people behind the scenes help the author get his ideas, structure his material, polish his style, edit his copy, and so forth.

I'd like to thank Isidore Friedman who taught me astrology and guided my later researches.

Marsha Kaplan, editor of *Astrology Guide* and *Your Personal Astrology*, who published my first literary efforts, and helped me channel my creative drive in constructive directions. Ehud and Lisa Sperling and Joan Ann DeMatia were tremendously helpful in organizing and editing the material. Pauline Bloom, my writing teacher, for her excellent workshops, and incisive grasp of literary technique.

My many astrologer friends, Nancy Dahlberg, Pete Peterson, Frank Don, Bobby and Aviva Greenbaum, and Greg Nielsen, whose hardheaded rap sessions yielded so many insights into the finer points of astrology.

Last, but not least, I'd like to thank my good friend Beatrice "Bibi" Wienstock who organized the typing of this manuscript in record time and with record thoroughness and accuracy.

Contents

Introduction 15

Part I

Chapter 1: Astrology: Facts, Fallacies, and
Fantasies 19

Chapter 2: Predestination and Free Will 26

Chapter 3: The Zodiac: A Natural Order of
Process 35

Part II

Introduction 47

Chapter 4: Making the Most of Your Sign 48

Chapter 5: Astroadvice for Consumers 58

Chapter 6: Astroguide to Better Communication 70

Chapter 7: Your Reading Habits and How to
Improve Them 86

Chapter 8: Relaxation Guide for the Signs ... 96

Chapter 9: Sex and the Signs 106

Chapter 10: How to Say "No" Nicely 121

Chapter 11: Planning Your Astrovacation 130

Chapter 12: Selling the Signs 139

Chapter 13: Living With the Signs 151

Part III

Introduction 167

Chapter 14: What Chart Patterns Can Tell You
at a Glance 177

Chapter 15: Elements and Human Behavior ... 192

Chapter 16: The Planets and Creativity 199

Chapter 17: The Practical Uses of the
Lunar Transits 208

Chapter 18: The Importance of the Qualities ... 214

Chapter 19: Future Studies 220

SUN SIGN
SUCCESS

Introduction

Estimates show that over 32 million Americans believe in astrology and that more than 80 percent of the American people know their Sun Signs. Every year the figures get higher. Yet besides being a conversation piece at parties and bars, what real use does this Sun Sign knowledge bring to the average person?

In this book I show practical ways in which you can take this elementary knowledge of your Sun Sign and convert it to practical benefit in many of the problems of everyday living.

For those of you whose knowledge of astrology is limited to only your Sun Sign, Parts I and II will be of special interest. Part III will best be understood by those of you who have had your charts done and have something to refer to. It will also be of special interest to those who know enough astrology to look up an ephemeris (a book which contains the positions of the planets for any given day) and actually experiment with the techniques described. Serious students of astrology will also benefit from this work because they will get some insights into many new practical areas of research.

A word about Sun Sign astrology: When we say that a person is an Aries or Taurus or Gemini, we mean that on the day of that person's birth the Sun was in a certain position in the heavens relative to the Earth. This position falls in one of the zodiacal signs, which are nothing more than mathematical divisions of the heavens. But the totality of a person's character depends on much more than just the Sun Sign. Remember there are nine other heavenly bodies in this solar system that relate with the Earth: the Moon and eight other planets. Each of these has a meaning in your horoscope. (A horoscope is a "map of the heavens" at birth, which contains not only the position of the Sun but also the nine other heavenly bodies.) The Sun's position, your Sun Sign, therefore, does not tell all about you by any means.

It *does* indicate, however, a few very important things. It shows the strength and the nature of your deepest inner urges and ambitions in life, and how you are likely to attain them. It shows your basic psychological attitude to life. The way you look at things—your viewpoint. It shows the nature and strength of your will power and your sense of individuality. And it shows the means and methods you must take to integrate all the forces of your being.

In this sphere, Sun Sign astrology is both valid and valuable. Nothing, of course, replaces having your chart done by a competent astrologer. This will open a whole new area of inner experience and understanding. And as I mentioned before, you will benefit even more from this book.

PART I

1

Astrology: Facts, Fallacies, and Fantasies

The popular conceptions of astrology are dreadful. People bandy around so many weird and ridiculous ideas in the name of astrology that it is no wonder many really intelligent people simply reject the whole study.

With many of my clients it is often necessary to spend considerable time in explaining what astrology *is not* before we can describe what it is. Very often we spend more time on the former than on the latter. Perhaps more than in any other field of study, the astrologer is confronted with people who have been told all kinds of lies about astrology either deliberately or through ignorance.

I would like to examine some of these popular conceptions in the light of astrological theory and explain their meaning or nonmeaning.

Predicting the Future

Predicting the future is a very misunderstood function and needs to be explored. People say that they don't believe in astrology because it purports to predict the future —which, of course is impossible—therefore, astrology must be humbug.

But what exactly do we mean by predicting the future? When the mathematician computes the positions of celestial bodies for the next thousand years, and he is well able to do it, is that not predicting the future? When the physicist computes that a rocket of such and such a structure, with X number of pounds of thrust, aimed at a certain angle and fired at a specific place and time will reach the Moon, is that not predicting the future? When the engineer states that if you hook up a battery, copper wire, and a lightbulb in a certain prescribed manner, a definite event will take place—the bulb will light up—is that not a prediction of the future?

Sure it is. Everything in the universe is governed by laws. Human behavior is also governed by laws: laws which are just as exact and binding as the laws of physics. If we knew these laws in the same way that the physicist or engineer knows his, and we were able to compute all the variables and account for them, we too could predict human behavior with rather good precision.

This, of course, is just theory. In practice, we don't know nearly enough about the laws of human behavior; even if we did, the incredible amount, the almost infinite number of variables that can effect future events is really beyond our scope. Thus if by predicting the future, we mean the computation of general trends which are based on the transiting, ever-shifting planetary powers and energies, then astrology is valid for that.

But if by prediction of the future we mean the foretelling of certain specific events for a person, country, or group, then astrology is definitely not valid. By specific events we mean things like: your mother will die in two weeks; or next Tuesday you will meet a tall, dark stranger who will sweep you off your feet, and so on. This kind of thing is beyond the scope of astrology, and astrology makes no claims whatever on this matter.

Astrology can only map, in diagram and symbolic form, the nature and intensity of the forces operative in nature and in people, but it cannot predict how a person will react to those forces.

Certain transits may indicate psychic storms or, perhaps, a drastic drop in a person's general energy level; it could produce a general irritability or weakness. To make a specific prediction based on this is merely guesswork. There are far too many variables to take into account.

There are times when the planetary energies are conducive for expansion on all levels; material, social, and financial. But that doesn't mean it will happen; that the person will automatically strike it rich or win a lottery or meet the man or woman of his or her dreams. All the astrologer can say is that this time is good for starting projects or expanding them. There will be a greater likelihood of success with anything done at this time.

Timing and phasing are vital for success in anything. A thing that fails at one time will succeed at another and vice-versa. No matter how skilled you are in your profession, or how good your ideas are, you will fail if your timing is off. Great men have often achieved their success, not so much because of any superiority in skill—there are always many unknowns who surpass them in this—but because they had a knack for seizing the right moment for action. And here astrology is valid.

There are some astrologers who do predict specific events, and it seems that they are often right. How do we explain this? Mere guesswork? Most probably not. Those who are able to predict with accuracy, and they are rare, owe this ability not to their astrological knowledge but to their psychic abilities. And psychism is beyond the scope of standard astrology.

Where Astrology is Most Valid

Astrology is most valid for learning about the structure of your physical, mental, and emotional makeup. Each of us is unique, and we're all structured differently. The horoscope shows in symbolic language what that structure is. Astrology, then, is a method for gaining self-knowledge. It is not the *only* method by any means. However, it is one of many valid methods, and it happens to work.

How much misery, suffering, and failure could be eliminated if parents knew a little astrology (they don't have to be scholars) in dealing with their children? It would be safe to say that the percentage of inmates in our prisons and mental institutions would drop drastically if this ever happened.

Daily we see parents of a particular sign and psychological structure treating their children, who very often are of completely different or opposite structures, as duplicates of themselves. A Cancerian mother cannot understand her Sagittarian son. He is a mystery and a trial to her and vice-versa. She can't understand his deep need for freedom or his dislike for the home. To her the home is her life, the very reason for her existence. "He must be crazy," she says, and then proceeds to teach him the right way to live and behave, or punishes him for being himself; for being true to his structure. Without a knowledge of astrology this mother and child are incomprehensible entities to each other. Their relationship must therefore be a destructive one.

How many marriages would be much happier if both parties understood each other's structure? If this were the case, the divorce rate would be cut drastically. All kinds of unreasonable demands, expectations, and fantasies about the other would be eliminated. A solid and stable relationship could then be built based on knowledge of facts and structure. This kind of a relationship has a much better chance to endure.

How many employees hate their jobs? Estimates indicate that over 80 percent of American workers don't like what they do. These figures are appalling and bode no good for the culture. When a person hates what he does, the quality of his work must suffer. And the quality of his health and inner feelings, too, must suffer. How is such a state of affairs allowed to occur? The mechanism of it is very simple.

A person, not knowing what he wants to do, takes a job temporarily until he finds himself. But since he has no idea what he is geared to do or what his natural abilities are, he falls into a job because of security. When he finally realizes what it is he'd like to do, it is usually too late; he has a family, or he's too old and doesn't have the energy and the drive to start something new.

Very often, it is better to follow a dream for which you have the structure to attain, even though it seems impractical, than to follow some safe and practical profession for which you have neither the structure nor the aptitude. According to Charles Luntz in his classic work *Vocational Astrology*, the really successful people in any field are the ones who *love* what they do. And though there are many moderately successful people doing what they dislike; had they been doing what they loved, they would have been much more successful, happier too.

In these areas of aptitudes, careers, and personal compatibility astrology is most valid. Here astrology becomes a practical and extremely effective tool for success.

On Belief

Many people ask me, "Do you really *believe* in astrology?" And then add, "I wish I could but I can't." The keyword in this question is the word *belief*. These people want to believe, they want to have faith in some system that will supply them with all the answers.

My answer usually is something like, "I don't believe in astrology either. I *know* it is valid. I *know* based on study, experiments, and experience. For what astrology claims to do, it does; it works."

Now, no really sincere astrologer wants anybody to believe in what he is saying or to accept astrological principles as a blind act of faith. It would be akin to asking somebody to believe in the laws of physics. Certain fields of study do not require or desire belief. To know about it, all you need to do is study its principles and test them, intelligently. If they work, well you've learned something, you know it. If they do not work, well, you discard them. But belief does not enter into the picture.

The astrologer is not looking for believers. He is looking for knowers—a big difference.

Which is the Best Sign?

Astrologers are always being asked, "Which is the best sign?" Or "I'm a Taurus. Is that any good?" It is amazing how many people walk around with the impression that there are good and bad signs, and that some signs are better or worse than others.

Each sign is a symbol for a function of nature. A person who is strong in a given sign will express the psychological attitude of the function. Each of these functions is equally important in the total scheme of things and the absence or the malfunction of *any* of these functions would seriously upset the balance and harmony of nature and could destroy the earth. All the signs, therefore, have something important to contribute.

To label any sign as good or bad is ridiculous. Each sign has a positive or negative mode of expression which depends on how its functions are used or misused. And this is dependent on us. The function itself is neutral.

When we express our functions negatively, it is we who are evil and not the sign.

The only way you can meaningfully talk about one sign of the zodiac being better than another is to talk about something specific. Some signs are better at handling certain jobs, situations, and life problems than others. A knowledge of this is important for the person choosing a career, a personnel manager who wants to hire the best possible applicant for a job, parents in dealing with children, and so on.

For example, *Earth signs* (Taurus, Virgo, Capricorn) are the best in business administration, organization, the handling of details, and material affairs. *Fire signs* are best (Aries, Leo, Sagittarius) for functions requiring energy, initiative, and courage. *Air signs* (Gemini, Libra, Aquarius) are the best communicators and planners of the zodiac. *Water signs* (Cancer, Scorpio, Pisces) are best at jobs that require imagination, sensitivity, and a sympathetic understanding of other people.

2

Predestination and Free Will

Is man really "the master of his fate—the captain of his soul"? Can he really create his own destiny? Or, is he a mere actor playing a script written long before he was born and about which he has no choice?

The predestination versus free will argument has raged for ages; and even today the vitriol shows little sign of weakening. There is as much confusion about it, as ever. If a poll were taken among astrologers, it would be a safe bet to guess that this is the question they are most frequently asked.

Let's examine both sides of the question. First let's define destiny. *Destiny* in its literal sense means "destination," or "goal." When we say someone has a certain destiny, we mean that he is going to a certain place, that is, he is headed in a specific direction. The cycle of his life and the nature of his actions serve to bring him closer to this goal. *Predestination* means that this destination is predetermined and the person has no choice in the matter. *Free will* means that a person's destiny is subject to his choice—his will.

The argument for predestination is not as absurd as it first appears. Aren't we all predestined to do many things? Once born, we must breathe, eat, sleep, grow, decay, and eventually die; we must earn a living, relate with others, and perform many actions which are distasteful to us. Even being born was not our choice. In our lives, we seem to spend much time dealing with outside factors—necessities not under our control. On the face of it, this sounds reasonable. But those who hold this view go further. They maintain that every minute act, every event which crops up is predestined. Your dinner last night was predestined, and so are all your future dinners. That I am writing this chapter and you are reading it is likewise predestined. They maintain that every action we make is the inexorable result of previous causes already set in motion; every new act brings into being chains of new causes which, in turn, will determine other actions, and so on and so forth, for eternity.

In short, man is securely bound to the wheel of his destiny by the chains of necessity. None can escape. The few who do were predestined to do it. This extreme view is held by many Protestant sects and by more than a few occultists. Only the predestined "chosen ones" can enter heaven.

Those who argue for free will maintain that man has the innate capacity to make choices. That his destiny and every action he takes is governed by these choices; and although many actions are caused by necessity, man nevertheless has the power to choose which necessities will be important to him and which of these he will allow to motivate his actions. Perhaps man cannot choose to be born, but he can certainly choose to die anytime he wants. Of a variety of possibilities man selects a profession, a home, a wife, a certain social sphere, and so on. He can change it anytime he wants.

27

Both sides have potent arguments. Like most burning issues of this sort neither side is completely right, nor is either side completely wrong. There are elements of truth and falseness in both arguments, and the answer, as usual, lies in the middle.

To the free willers we can ask: can man *really* do anything he chooses? Is their contention supported by actual life-facts, by empirical observation of life experience? Can a man, for example, choose to bear a child? Can a middle-aged 90-pound weakling choose to become a pro football player? Can a moron of subnormal intelligence choose to become a philosopher? What of all those born with physical defects; can they choose to do anything they want? Aren't certain professions, for which the cost of training is high, closed to a poor person who must go out and work at an early age? What of the innumerable situations that crop up over which one man can have no control: job layoffs, financial panics, wars, famine, death? Life experience seems to show many situations which cannot be controlled and which dictate their own necessary actions independent of a person's will.

To the predestinationers we can ask: Is man *really* devoid of any choice at all? Is he really just a helpless cork on a raging sea of necessity? How do life facts bear out this view? Can I not choose to lift my arm or drop it if I so desire? Can I not close my eyes or open them of my own free will? Isn't it my choice whether I go out to the movies or stay home, or walk around the block or play cards with my friends? Life seems to be full of choices. The beautiful girl who chooses one beau out of a host of many admirers, the student who chooses one career out of many possibilities, the scientist who chooses a specific area of research, the writer who writes on a specific subject, can we really say that all these actions are predestined?

Obviously, the issues here are very complex and cut and dried answers will not suffice. I would like to explain the esoteric view of this question, with the understanding that this explanation is far from complete.

We all have within us in varying degrees of development, a Higher Self. Different traditions and different teachers have labeled it according to their beliefs. Some call it the Spirit, the Spiritual Ego, the Divine Spark, the Monad, the Ruach, the Being, the I AM, the Noetic Self, the Christos, the Individuality—whatever label we choose to give it, it is maintained that this is who and what we really are. Our personality or psyche is merely a projection or a reflection of this Real Self.

In astrological symbolism it is the Sun. This is the part of us that is immortal—that sheds bodies and personalities like suits of old clothes. The Real Self incarnates (is born into) in a body for the purpose of gaining experiences through which new aptitudes and abilities will be developed; these are necessary for its further growth. When we die, all our experiences are reviewed and digested by the Higher Self. Those lessons we have learned well, the new abilities and aptitudes we have developed and mastered, are incorporated into it. These become part of its "spiritual capital," and can be used by the Being.

There are, however, many lessons we have not learned; many abilities we have not acquired. The Higher Self will look at these weaknesses, assess them, and decide the best way to correct them in the next incarnation. The Being will not incarnate until space-time conditions are exactly right for learning of those lessons. The physical body and the personality it selects will be those that are best equipped to learn those lessons. All these factors ensure that certain experiences will be attracted to the life of the personality.

In this way, loosely speaking, a certain part of our lives is predestined. We are born into certain physical, mental, emotional, social, and financial conditions which will attract definite life events into our lives. A Being may incarnate in a certain country, in a certain race and family, in time of war and depression, or in time of peace; it may select a rich family or a slum family, no matter, any of these factors will attract experiences and have tremendous impact on the development of the personality. So although in a sense we are actors, nevertheless, it is we who wrote the script; and although many negative outside events are predestined, we do have free will in the handling of them and more importantly in our *inner* reactions to them.

A person's inner development and growth is subject to his free will. The proper inner attitude to things is the first step in mastering outside events. Man has free will but is yet predestined. Like many enigmas about man, the answer lies in circularity. We are born into a certain predestined set of outside circumstances which we can master by exercising will over our inner selves. This eventually brings a whole new spate of outer circumstances with its positives and negatives. These will demand new inner reactions, and these will bring new events, and so on.

An example: Three boys are born into poor families and raised in the slums. Because of this each of them was born with certain predestined handicaps. They had to scrounge for food, there was no money for education, and they were not exposed to any of the so-called finer things. Each of these boys reacted differently to this predestined handicap, the result being that each had a different destiny.

One, so beaten down by conditions and hardships, gave up hope. He accepted his condition bitterly and blamed everyone else for it. He was angry and resentful—but he never did anything to get out of the slums. So he stayed there, an embittered man with no hope, working at a job far below his real potential. He married a woman who was as embittered as he was, and they raised two embittered children, who had a good chance of duplicating their father's destiny.

The second boy, resentful of the many things he lacked, did determine to do something about it. He decided to work on his outside limitations without working or training any inner faculties, such as skills, abilities, aptitudes. He felt that money was the answer, that money alone could fill the void of his previous deprivations. So he set out to get it. But not having any skills, there was no honest way he could make it. He turned to a life of crime, and acquired the destiny that accompanies such a life. Like a hurricane or a flood, he became a negative force in the environment—creating it and evoking it in others wherever he went. There was no way he could avoid attracting negativity to himself.

The third boy also determined to do something about his predicament. He, too, felt very keenly the deprivations he was forced to endure. But he chose a different way of escape. He began to explore himself and his potential. He did not resent present circumstances, but instead used the discomfort of them to spur his efforts. He went to school at night, read voraciously on many different subjects, and tried his hand at many skills.

He finally decided that his gifts were in music. For years, he worked at the craft diligently, painstakingly. He trained his mind and body to play the piano. He spent every spare penny on lessons and sheet music. Every day he worked toward his goal until he was good enough to play professionally.

In doing what he loved and what suited his nature, he did not resent the long hours of practice. He loved it. He wanted to learn as much as he could about it, and perhaps break new ground and enrich the art by personal achievement. By changing his inner state he had changed outer conditions. He exchanged the destiny of a poor slum boy to that of a great musician. Naturally, this life also has its problems, and he would have to develop new inner abilities to master them. But the important thing was that he was growing. He was using his free will to develop himself.

Maurice Nicole is fond of saying that "Your state of being attracts your life." By this I think he means that we attract what we are. Our inner states, attitudes, and

31

qualities determine what happens to us. If we are chaotic and negative inside, like a magnet we attract those kinds of events. But change the inner state, and you have literally changed your destiny.

There are, however, events that occur which are really beyond the control of any person, no matter how developed he is. We live among others, in a certain country, in a certain race of people, as individuals we share all the problems of the group. Technically, this is known as *group* or *race karma*. Whatever happens to the group affects every individual in one way or another.

Some good examples of this are the current financial and energy crises, inflation, and racial discrimination. Solving these kinds of problems is really beyond the scope of any one person even if he is president of the U.S. It is a group problem and only the cooperation of the group can solve it. The individual, however, can still choose his personal way of dealing with these problems. He has complete free will in his reaction to it.

In his personal way he can elect to deal with it constructively or destructively. He can get angry, molest gas station attendants, demand a revolution, and further worsen the problems, or he can use it as a learning experience to sharpen his faculties, to find ingenious creative ways of surmounting the difficulty. In Isidore Friedman's book *Organics: The Law of Breathing Spiral*, there is a quote from the ancient Egyptian mysteries: "Gather the forces sent against you, recognize them as necessary for your evolution, and turn them to your advantage." In this way problems become exercises that strengthen creative skills.

The astrological approach, although not conflicting with the standard occult view of predestination, is much simpler and easier to understand.

What is a horoscope anyway? It is a diagram or a blueprint that outlines your *basic structure*. It shows the ingredients and their relationships that have gone in to making you what you are. This is predestined and outside our control. You can modify and improve the structure, that is, make it more efficient and perhaps bring it to its highest possible development and expression. This is the province of the will. On the human level the will can only operate within the structural limitations of the person. A man cannot decide to bear a child; he is not structured to do it. A middle-aged, 90-pound body is simply not structured to take the punishment that goes with being a pro football player. So again, we see that man is influenced by both predestination and free will.

Some more examples of this: A typewriter is built along certain fixed lines and designed to do a certain kind of work. You could say it is predestined to type; it cannot do anything else. But what it types and the quality of what it can produce are practically infinite. It can type hate letters or business correspondence, pornography or poetry; lies or truths. The typewriter *must* be a typewriter, but what it types and how it types are subject to free will.

A stove is built for cooking, but what gets cooked is subject to choice. Similarly, a strong Piscean nature is structured along certain lines. Within his structure he has free will to express himself in many ways. He can be a poet or an idler, an artist or a drug addict, but there is no way he can become a Capricorn, which is a completely different structure. He is predestined to be a Pisces. Perhaps if he works on himself, he can incorporate certain Capricornian traits in himself, and he could become, through training, a practical Pisces. But never could he become a Capricorn. If he tried to impose that kind of life on himself, he would get pretty sick.

Here, perhaps lies one of the greatest uses of astrology. For in outlining structure, it shows your limits. It shows what things you must simply accept about yourself and what areas you can change. Where the use of free will is likely to have its best results and where you are butting your head against a wall. Most of our problems stem from trying to be something we are not, and from not being what we could and should be. Every sign has many levels of expression. Whatever sign we happen to be, we can strive to express its highest form. Here is where the will can do something.

3

The Zodiac: A Natural Order of Process

When the late astrological genius, Grant Lewi, was asked why he believed in astrology, his blunt answer was "I believe in it because it works." This is as good an answer as any; and there is no doubt that Mr. Lewi could have elaborated had he felt like it. (His two astrological works *Astrology for the Millions* and *Heaven Knows What* are classics.) However, there are many people who are dissatisfied with this type of answer and are searching for a deeper understanding of astrological principles. To these people we say that astrology works because it is based on natural law. It involves the study of forces which are as basic as electricity and magnetism. It charts basic elementary processes that are not limited to one field but rather are universal in scope. These processes are going on around us all the time.

Even the biggest skeptic has to admit, if he is at all conscious, that everything he sees, nature, people, animals, plants, organizations, machines, relationships, constantly goes through cycles of birth, growth and development, maturity, decline and death. This is basic and readily observable. The astrologer studies these processes as they relate to man or groups of men. *The signs of the zodiac are symbolical representations of different stages of this natural process; each sign is a different phase in the cycle.*

Although, approached much differently, these natural cycles are studied by zoologists in relation to animals; by botanists in relation to plants; by historians in relation to civilizations; by management consultants in relation to business, and so on in each field. *Astrological symbolism, if rightly understood, could be applied to all these disciplines*—for everything in nature begins with an Aries stage and progresses to the Taurus stage, then the Gemini stage, and on through each of the twelve signs.

To explain, let's trace the development of a business enterprise in terms of astrological symbolism. Let's see how its natural cycle of growth corresponds to the natural stages, charted by the zodiacal signs.

1. *The Aries Stage*

John Jones, a longtime executive at a "widget" plant, has an idea for a new type of "widget" which will revolutionize the industry. This first stage is the *initial creative impulse*, primitive, raw, undefined. He's all excited about the idea and decides to go into business for himself. *Impulsively*, perhaps, he leaves his present job to work on his project.

2. *The Taurus Stage*

At this point, Jones realizes that before he can go any further, he must bring his idea "down to earth." He must build an actual working model of his widget. What is the most practical way of manufacturing it? What materials or substances should it be made out of? How much money will it cost? These are some of the concerns of this phase. The creative impulse of Aries must now be channeled in a *practical, productive* way. Mere enthusiasm and energy is not enough; an actual, working widget has to be produced; and once produced, it must be patented and protected by law so that Jones can say, *"It's mine—I own it."* After this is accomplished, Jones must proceed to the next stage, if he wants his dream to come true.

3. *The Gemini Stage*

Now Jones finds that he must do some rudimentary *planning*. He must *gather facts* about plant space, hiring employees, and financial assistance. He must begin to *communicate* his idea with others. He has to interview prospective employees, sell the bankers on his idea, negotiate with landlords, buy equipment, and gather data on the competition. In short, he must begin to deal in an *active* and *flexible* way with different aspects of the public. He has to put himself in communication with the outside world. If he has done this well and is successful, he can proceed further.

4. *The Cancer Stage*

Now the company is born. Like an infant, however, it needs *protection and nourishment* from internal sources. In a sense it is still in the womb. It is not yet self-sufficient. Time, money, and energy must be supplied from Jones and his backers. At this stage the company begins to *establish roots*. It has an address at home. *Traditions are started; loyalties are pledged.* The company takes on the aspects of a fledgling family with Jones as both father and mother.

This is a crucial period. For if the roots are not sunk deep enough, if everyone doesn't pull together like a *family*, if there is disloyalty or a lack of *tenacity and resourcefulness*, then the company will die stillborn from the pressures of the harsh competitive world. A company, like a baby, cannot be protected artificially forever. Customers must be sought. Once found, they must be held *possessively* and persuaded, at all costs, to stay within the fold. Competitive pricing, attractive terms, hard sell, soft sell, anything to attract the customer and keep him. If this stage is successfully completed, the company (American Widgets) is ready for the fifth stage.

5. *The Leo Stage*

Now the company must establish its own *individuality*. American Widgets must be unique; there are no others like them. "American Widgets are the best!" "American Widgets are the leaders in the field" In order for the company to leave the "womb" and compete in the marketplace, it has to strengthen its image. President Jones spends thousands of dollars, wining and dining customers, advertising, selling, pushing. With the orders streaming in, the company has to *really* produce. And produce it does. Widgets fly off the assembly line in steady streams. The company is functioning at its full creative capacity. All orders are accepted indiscriminately. But nobody cares—the first rush of success is too exhilarating. And if the company loses a few dollars on bad credit risks, bankruptcy, wastage, or inefficiency, who cares? It is making up for it in other areas.

6. *The Virgo Stage*

The creative surge cannot last. As time goes on President Jones finds that the company is out of balance. The increase in production and sales necessitates hiring and training new workers, and purchasing new equipment. He also finds that his widgets need *servicing*. He must now set up a new department to service all the widgets that he sells. He is losing too much money on bad orders, poor credit risks. He must set up a department to *analyze* and check all incoming orders, to weed out the good from the bad. In short, he must take stock. He must *study and analyze* the whole structure of the company and set up *practical, efficient systems* to handle all the *details* and new problems that seem to arise everyday.

On the production line, *quality control* must be instituted so that only high quality widgets are shipped. The others must be thrown out. These are the challenges of the Virgo phase after he has

1. Set up a system for analyzing credit orders
2. Set up a system for hiring and training new workers
3. Set up a quality control system for production
4. Set up a service department
5. Set up a system for handling details

He can then enter into the seventh stage.

7. *The Libra Stage*

In this stage he must first balance all these various departments and functions so that his internal operation runs smoothly. American Widgets can now compete in the marketplace in a balanced way. The going is smooth. Growth is steady but not wild. Profits are respectable. The company is secure. President Jones joins many trade organizations and community groups. American Widgets becomes known as a respected company with enlightened views of its role in community affairs. A tactful public relations firm is hired to spread the word of the company's activities in the community. President Jones manages to negotiate two brilliant *merger* deals in which American

Widgets maintains control. This stage becomes the businessman's paradise, nothing much to worry about except where to invest the profits, the company image, and some minor interoffice political squabbles.

8. *The Scorpio Stage*

"The honeymoon is over; Adam is chased out of paradise." National Widgets, American Widgets' largest competitor, has come up with a widget that is equal, if not superior, to American's item. National Widget is pushing it with a massive sales and public relations campaign. For American Widgets the choice is clear and unmistakable. It can stay as it is and gradually wither and die, or it can mobilize its full resources of brains, energy, and determination to do two things: First, American Widgets can bring to light its reason for existing, namely its original widget; and second, it can study the item and research it from all angles. Then it can either *transform and improve it* or *eliminate* it completely and develop an entirely new item, superior in all respects to National's item.

This is the crossroads for the company: it must either *regenerate* or *degenerate*—do or die. It is a battle for survival and the stakes are high. *It can soar to the heights or sink to the depths.* There is no in between.

President Jones meets the challenge with intense vigor and determination. For months he and a staff of research engineers focus their energies on the task, and are finally successful. American Widgets announces the development of the "Widget II," the finest widget available, based on a newly discovered process of widgetry. In a sense the company is *reborn*.

9. *The Sagittarius Stage*

American Widgets begins to push the new item. A massive sales campaign begins and is very successful. The company starts to *expand* at a tremendous rate. New plants are built. *Plans for expansion* into foreign countries are drawn up and discussed. President Jones decides to become an international firm.

The new process of widget making has opened up new vistas in the industry. *Ideas* for new products based on this process are flowing across President Jones' desk. *The ideas seem limitless*—expansion is unending. American Widgets (AMWID) is the hottest growth stock on the market. President Jones and his entire executive staff are *jovial and beaming optimistically*.

10. *The Capricorn Stage*

The company's problems at this point stem from abundance. There are too many ideas, too much expansion: If American Widgets is to remain healthy, it must begin to set *limits* for itself. It must decide on a few products and focus on them. It must take the best of the innumerable new ideas and choose the most practical and profitable of these. If the company's expansion is to remain stable, it must become more efficient. Only the most profitable plants should be kept in operation, the others should be closed down. Foreign expansion should be limited to those countries which are the most profitable and have stable governments and economies.

An international recession may come and all the "fat must be trimmed," sometimes ruthlessly. The internal organization of the company, with all its branches, must be restructured and ordered to maximize profits. High-priced efficiency experts, Saturnian, ruthlesss looking men, are hired to oversee this phase. They do their job well and American Widgets becomes the number one widget maker in the country.

11. *The Aquarius Stage*

American Widgets begins to have a *universal outlook* and flavor. A board of directors meeting is almost like a

U.N. meeting. The company renames itself, "International Widgets." President Jones (now Chairman Jones) and his executives are now very concerned with world affairs since anything that happens almost anywhere in the world affects the company.

The company's major decisions are no longer made by him alone. Now all decisions are made by *groups* of high executives. It is management by committee. Everything has become systematized and institutionalized, from the planning function to research and development. Chairman Jones, now a powerful world figure, can only operate with the advice and consent of his committees and executives. He cannot afford to alienate them.

12. *The Pisces Stage*

The long uphill battle for success has taken its toll of Chairman Jones and many of his long-time faithful executives. They are tired and, to tell the truth, bored. The Company in which they so joyfully and energetically put most of their lives into creating has now become almost a prison. Some retire, some stay out of a sense of duty. There is no challenge any more, and Chairman Jones spends much time watching, with wry amusement, younger executives jockeying for power.

He is so bored that he fails to notice that Dan Smith, Manager of Plant Engineering, has resigned from the company to start his own business. Rumor has it that he has just invented a "Super Widget" that will make everything on the market obsolete. Chairman Jones, doesn't even bother to check this rumor out, he's just very amused.

Of course, this is a very simplistic outline, but it does give a general idea of the processes involved. Many companies falter at one of the stages and do not make it through the rest. Many individuals fail to meet the challenges of each stage of this process, too. But the zodiac does show the next step and the problems it contains. Understanding the zodiacal signs is a great tool for a deeper and better understanding of the processes and developments that are taking place in, and around us, continually and eternally.

PART II

Introduction

The following chapters are designed to show you how to take one basic piece of raw datum and apply it to some of the problems we all confront in daily living. Remember, we said that the Sun Sign indicates your psychological attitude to life. Just this fact alone must have important consequences in how you handle people and situations. It must affect every area of your life not just the few that we mention here.

If you keep in mind that in reality, man is an organism-as-a-whole, it will be axiomatic that every factor in a person's psychic structure must affect every other factor. We will go deeper into the concept of the organism-as-a-whole in later chapters. In the meantime, try to apply some of the knowledge in these chapters and see the difference it makes in handling yourself and others.

4

Making the Most of Your Sign

Each sign of the zodiac represents a basic psychological attitude—a certain unique way of looking at and dealing with the world. Each sign has certain unique strengths and weaknesses. When an astrologer does your chart, he tries to give you an understanding of these strengths and weaknesses so that you will be able to see the first more effectively and begin to eliminate the second.

Paradoxically, it seems that many of our problems are not always caused by lacks or overt weaknesses in our character, but rather the reverse. We create problems by misusing or overusing our *strengths*. We so overemphasize our positive qualities that we create imbalances in ourselves. My teacher used to call this phenomenon "the negatives of the positive."

It is analagous to a man with a very well-developed right leg. He tries to use his right leg all the time because it is so much better, and he has so much more control over it. So he ignores his left leg and keeps developing the right one. After a while his right leg is very strong and more well developed than before, yet he finds that he has trouble walking; his left leg has atrophied and he is now off balance.

Another example: The main problem with Aries is not so much that he is weak on details; he is not really expected to be strong in this area because it is outside of his structural coordinates. In fact, the Aries should avoid jobs in which this is a requirement. His main problem stems within the positives of his own nature. His gift and power to start new things, to pioneer, to act forcefully gets out of his control. He becomes rash, impulsive, and self-centered.

Similarly, the Virgo, because of his analytical and critical strengths eats up details. His problem is not that he doesn't have the pioneering drive of the Aries, but rather that he misuses his positives. He overanalyzes, overcriticizes, and gets too caught up in details. Nobody expects him to be a pioneer—it is outside of his function.

No matter what our sign is, we must make the most of it. And making the most of it quite often means learning to control and balance our positives so that they don't become negative through misuse.

A useful technique through which this can be accomplished is as follows: Whatever sign you are, begin to study, understand, and build into your nature the positive qualities of your opposite sign. This procedure will almost automatically begin to balance your nature.

There are many astrologers who believe that the signs are only comprehensible when viewed in connection with their opposites. Each sign is merely one aspect of a duality. And, they say, that the zodiac should be viewed as six pairs of polar opposites in which each opposite complements the other. The six zodiacal opposites are

1. Aries (Mar. 21–Apr. 20)	Libra (Sept. 24–Oct. 23)
2. Taurus (Apr. 21–May 21)	Scorpio (Oct. 24–Nov. 22)
3. Gemini (May 22–June 21)	Sagittarius (Nov. 23–Dec. 21)
4. Cancer (June 22–July 23)	Capricorn (Dec. 22–Jan. 20)
5. Leo (July 24–Aug. 23)	Aquarius (Jan. 21–Feb. 19)
6. Virgo (Aug. 24–Sept. 23)	Pisces (Feb. 20–Mar. 20)

According to these astrologers it is impossible to for a person to reach the highest expression of his sign unless he learns the lesson of its opposite. So the Arian must become more Libran, and the Scorpio must become more Taurean, and so on. Let's analyze the lessons of the opposites:

Aries—Libra

As mentioned, the Arian is endowed with a powerful drive and urge for activity, especially new activity. His basic function, cosmically, is that of the pioneer and leader. If we study history, we find that almost every major step of human progress was the result of the pioneering efforts of an individual. It is only later, perhaps when the person is dead, that others come along and develop and improve on his innovation. This drive and push that is capable of overcoming the heavy initial resistance that always block new endeavors is Aries. This kind of force must be self-centered and self-contained—a lot of power must be generated. But if this drive gets out of control, you have an impulsive, rash, and impatient person who is insufferable to be with and who will ride roughshod over others. This can be very destructive.

The Aries, therefore, should learn the lessons of its opposite sign Libra. Libra is the sign of balance and the sign that rules the relationship principle. Whereas Aries is concerned primarily with the self, Libra is concerned with others. Whereas Aries sees his own viewpoint, Libra sees both sides of the picture. When Aries' actions are blind, hot, and enthusiastic, Libra's are cool, planned, and calculated. Aries does first and thinks later; Libra thinks first and does later.

Any Aries, who can balance his drive for action with cool, and reasoned thought and who can see the viewpoint of others as clearly as he sees his own, will be making the most of his sign. The combination is extremely powerful and very hard to beat.

The Libran must do the reverse. The positive qualities of Libra when misused, lead to vacillation, laziness, and an inability to make decisions. They become overly refined and lack a sense of self. Worst of all, they tend to look for their center in other people.

Libra must, therefore, develop some of the Arian's sense of self, and learn how to act in a forceful manner. They must develop a little of the Arian's capacity for hard work and especially the Arian's intestinal fortitude. Libra should also learn from Aries to resist the urge to always compromise and to stand on their own principles when necessary.

Taurus—Scorpio

The Taurean is characterized by an intense need for material security. This gives him the natural ability to stabilize and make things permanent on the physical plane. He can take nebulous ideas and put them into form. He has a natural ability for making money and understands the need for a stable and secure environment. He is fully capable of making this happen. This is a great strength. When this gets out of hand, though, it degenerates into the blind urge to acquire and possess. All his practical abilities will be harnessed to this end—to the exclusion and denigration of anything else.

To make the most of his abilities, Taurus must learn some of the lessons of Scorpio. When Taurus is blindly acquiring more and more things, Scorpio is eliminating the essentials. Taurus is mainly concerned with physical things, whereas Scorpio is trying to penetrate into the deeper secrets of life. When Taurus is using his practical abilities solely to increase his own possessions, Scorpio is using his considerable practical abilities in service of others, in managing the possessions of others.

When Taurus can see past the material world, when he learns to eliminate unnecessary things, when he begins to probe into life a little deeper, then he is making the most of his sign.

Scorpio is characterized by a powerful intensity and focus on his desires. This is a great asset since focus, concentration, and the elimination of nonessentials is the keynote to success in any field. His intensity and seriousness may get out of hand and could make him a fanatic. He can put people off by "coming on too strong." He has to learn some of Taurus' venusian amiability. Before the Scorpio tries to manage the possessions of others, he should, of course, first learn how to handle his own—the lesson of Taurus.

Gemini—Sagittarius

The Gemini's strong point is his strong intellect and his gift for fluent communication. His communication deals with the everyday concerns of life and without it society could not exist. His problem is that his love for amassing data and information gets out of control, and we have a person who is a walking encyclopedia of unrelated, uncoordinated, and unorganized facts which serve no real purpose. They can get too caught up in masses of superficial knowledge with no long-term or serious import, for the information is not related into a coherent structure.

To really be able to make the most of his intellect, Gemini should look to Sagittarius for guidance. Sagittarius deals with long-term communication; that is, information of serious import for society as a whole, knowledge that is organized into a philosophical or metaphysical structure that can endure and be improved on.

Gemini is the untrained intellect endowed only with its native abilities and primarily geared to deal with the immediate environment. Sagittarius is the trained intellect, the intellect that has been forced as a tool, an intellect that can be used to *expand* the person's sphere of influence beyond the immediate environment. Gemini learns by direct perception, by inspiration. Gemini sees only the immediate; Sagittarius sees the future. Gemini is concerned mainly with the concrete; Sagittarius with the ideal. Gemini, therefore, must widen and train his intellect and make of it a proper tool.

Sagittarius, on the other hand, tends to get lost in his visions of the ideal and to almost completely ignore the concrete—the everyday details of life. He gets lost in the wide vistas of his inspiration and very often lacks the raw data, the facts needed to prove his inspirations so that they can be communicated to others. The highest abstract truths when applied in particular situations must undergo certain modifications, sometimes these modifications are drastic. Do these abstract truths that he sees actually apply in everyday life? Does the mass of data available tend to prove his inspiration or disprove it? As a rule the Sagittarian doesn't care. He needs some Gemini traits to round out and make proper use of his inspirations. Sagittarius has tendencies of getting too hot and excited and overly optimistic about his ideas. He should learn Gemini's cool and matter of fact attitude to balance off. The Sagittarian vision and the Geminian communication need each other.

Cancer—Capricorn

The Cancer is concerned with the home and with his deepest gut-level feelings. His strong point is his intense urge to nourish and protect those he loves. This, too, is a very important function and without it we couldn't survive. Without a strong and stable home, a strong society is impossible.

When the Cancer's urge to nourish and protect gets out of hand, it becomes overprotection and "smother love." The home becomes a prison that stifles loved ones rather than protecting them. The warm Cancerian feelings can degenerate into total absorption in the home and personal matters. It is their children, their home, their friends, their tribe, that is important, completely ignoring outer, objective concerns. They imprison and are themselves imprisoned in the womb of the subconscious instincts.

It is essential that they learn some of the Capricornian traits to balance off. Cancer is emotional; Capricorn is mental. Cancer is personal and subjective; Capricorn is impersonal and objective. Cancer is concerned with the past; Capricorn with the future. Cancer is concerned only with the home; Capricorn is concerned with the career and serving the public. Cancer's interests are narrow, whereas Capricorn's are, of necessity, wider.

Cancer must learn that without discipline and cool measurement a home life is impossible. A home cannot run on raw emotion alone, it needs efficiency and craftsmanship, too.

For the Capricorn the reverse is true. His strong point is discipline, duty, and efficiency spurred by a driving ambition to establish a solid image before the public and a stable material base. He has emotions, but they are so sternly repressed that he can be quite ruthless and cold to others, while in pursuit of his career. This drive can cause him to neglect domestic concerns as unimportant, or he will fulfill them out of a sense of duty. He has to learn some of Cancer's warmth and good feeling. He has to learn that a stable home is equally as important as a career. He has to get more in touch with his deeper feelings and learn how to express them properly.

Leo—Aquarius

Leo's strong point is his overabundance of life force and creative power. The Leo is well aware of this power and is always seeking to express it; it would be hard indeed to keep that kind of power inside. Like the Sun which is his planetary ruler, his energy is such that it is always trying to affect the environment rather than be affected by it. His natural bent is leadership, which in itself is a very positive quality. The one thing a society needs is good leaders.

But when the Leo cannot control his creative energies, he seeks leadership in all things even in areas for which he is not qualified by training or ability. He becomes hot, flamboyant, and reckless. He has trouble relating with groups in the right way. He gets so caught up in his individuality that he cannot recognize the individuality of others. Like the Sun he thinks himself the center of a solar system and others exist to express his grandeur.

To make the most of his sign, Leo must look to Aquarius and develop his impersonal, detached mental outlook. This will cool off some of the hot fires of his creative energies and give them a wider range of expression. He must learn from the Aquarian that an individual cannot exist without a group. He must serve it and integrate into it.

The Aquarian, on the other hand, must look to Leo for the force and the drive to put his ideas and theories into action. The Aquarian also tends to overemphasize the group to the exclusion of the individual. He must learn that humanitarian ideals cannot exist without free individuals. Before you can have the brotherhood of man, you must have the manhood of the brother; the lesson of Leo. Aquarian ideals cannot manifest with just any group; they require a group of *individuals*.

Aquarians, being the strongest of the mental signs, are

apt to get trapped in theories and ideas rather than action. This trait they must get from Leo.

Virgo—Pisces

Virgo's greatest strength is his ability to analyze and differentiate, the ability to recognize and handle details, the ability to take a large complex subject and break it into small, manageable parts. This makes him very hardheaded, practical and efficient.

Pisces' greatest strength is the opposite. His gift is synthesis; the ability to see wholes; to see the unity behind things, to see relationships and connections between things. He tends to ignore differences and see the similarities between things. His vision is wide and his sympathies are deep.

Virgo sees infinite detail; Pisces sees infinite space. These two signs are like looking at the world through two radically different instruments—a telescope and a microscope. The Virgo looks at reality through a microscope. He sees every detail and the finest shades of difference. The Pisces perceives reality through a telescope. He sees far and he sees wide. Details get lost in the vistas of overall patterns. Yet, both these signs are complementary. They need each other.

When Virgo's powers of analysis get out of hand, he becomes nit-picky, petty and exacting on himself and others. He analyzes so much that he ignores the whole picture. Analysis by itself is meaningless and destructive. To be really effective it must take place in a field of synthesis. Before you can begin to analyze, you must have some idea of the whole picture. Virgo's urge for perfection makes him overly critical and intolerant of his less efficient fellows. He needs some of the Piscean's sympathies and compassion.

Pisces' wide vision and ultrahigh idealism can put him in a dream world to the exclusion of taking care of his everyday life which is so important for success. Practical things are very boring when contrasted with his visions of the future. These attributes he must learn from Virgo. A strong intuition is very important in creative work, but if you are driving a car, or handling equipment, or doing any of the ordinary mundane tasks of life, then you had better be aware of details. This is one of the most important lessons that Pisces has to learn: He has to know how, when, and where to use his intuition.

When the analytical and practical abilities of Virgo are combined with the vision and the understanding of Pisces, we have one of the strongest combinations in the zodiac.

5

Astroadvice For Consumers

In a society in which money is so ardently worshipped, financial success, very often, is merely the measure of a man's greed. Society feeds this greed by defying those whose only virtue is a large bank balance. How this bank balance was acquired is of very little importance. Criminality is thus very subtly nurtured in the very structures of the race mind. And though society can point to all kinds of laws which expressly forbid criminality, and though it can point to prisons full of people convicted of violating these laws, it blithely continues to create the atmosphere wherein more criminals, victims, laws, and jails are produced.

Criminality is not really punished. It is *unsuccessful* criminality that is punished. Successful criminals, those who are not caught, become folk heros, people to be envied and emulated. Books, movies, and TV specials depict their rise to success.

In a society such as this it is not surprising that problems like consumer fraud exist. What is surprising is that so many reputable businessmen and businesses do exist. In a hostile atmosphere in which "wheeler-dealerism" is the order of the day, this is nothing short of a miracle.

It would seem safe to speculate that there isn't one of us who, at one time or other, has not been victimized by consumer fraud. It is perhaps the most rampant form of crime in our culture. Contractors, plumbers, and electricians charge high prices, very often pad their bills, and do shoddy work that doesn't last. For years the public has been victimized by phoney contractors who would take a deposit and never come back. Many repair shops, automobile, radio, and TV, also pad their bills outrageously. What's more, it is almost impossible to prove. Insurance salesmen get raises and bonuses for selling people insurance that they very often don't need. Frozen fish dealers soak their fish in water before freezing them so that all this extra weight is added to the price you pay.

The other day I heard a story of a butcher who puts metal weights into the tail of the chickens and turkeys he sells to add to the weight which therefore raises the price. Most people don't eat the tails and so they never notice.

Thousands of people are swindled every year by men who accost them on a busy street and show them a famous brand watch, or some jewelry in a famous name box, and tell them that they can sell it real cheap because it's "hot." They are experts in creating an air of urgency and secrecy and pressuring the pedestrian to buy. Very often he does, thinking that he's got a bargain and later finds that the merchandise is phoney and worthless. The seller melts into the crowd unnoticed and makes more sales.

There are undoubtedly many more schemes that I've never heard of, and many more than could be enumerated here. Are more laws and more committees and protection agencies the answer? I don't think so. Although these factors are somewhat of a help, their real action is to suppress symptoms and not to strike at causes. A man-made law never solved anything, permanently, at least. What man can make, man can find ways to break. Rather than more laws, we need more awareness, more perception, more knowledge, and more consciousness on the part of the general public. For the causes, dear Brutus lie not with the criminals but within our own breasts. It is our lack of awareness that allows us to be cheated. More awareness and consciousness on our part is the only factor that can effect any real and permanent change.

Like any other carnivore and predator, the con men exist only because their prey is abundant. Let the supply of gullible and unaware people drop in a drastic way, and these con men would be as extinct as the dinosaur.

Kahil Gibran has said, "For every murder the victim is to blame." At first glance the great poet seems to be talking nonsense. But if we give it some thought, we get a glimmer of understanding. Nothing can happen to you that is not a part of your psyche. Events that occur on the outside are attracted by certain tunings and weaknesses in the psyche; we are like magnets that attract the iron filings of events. So even when an innocent man is murdered, there had to be weakness and unconsciousness within him that allowed or even caused that event to happen.

So it is with consumer fraud. There are certain factors in a horoscope which indicate a person's susceptibility to frauds of all kinds. These have to do with planetary placements by sign, and house, and with the aspects (angular relationships) between planets in a birth chart. This kind of analysis is beyond the scope of this book, which deals with basic Sun Sign data.

Yet there is much that your Sun Sign can tell you about your attitude to fraud. A strong Piscean nature, for example, has to be particularly on its guard here. They are prone to desires, impulses, goals, and thoughts, that are formless, vague, and nebulous. The native is likely to be a dreamer, an idealist, who looks at the world through rose-colored glasses. An untrained Pisces is very likely to make purchases without any discrimination or prior thought. They are much too sensitive to the feelings and desires of others even when these desires can prove harmful to them. This very often makes them an easy mark for a strong, glib, high-pressure salesman. The easy going Piscean temperament makes the native particularly fascinated with the temptation to earn easy money fast. And this is the main motive that a con man appeals to in a mark. Learning to be practical and down-to-earth is one of the Piscean's main life lessons.

He should avoid any venture that is not totally legitimate and above board. He should avoid making any kind of long-term or speculative investment without consulting two or more trusted friends, preferably Capricorns, and researching the whole thing thoroughly. Even when shopping for everyday things, the Pisces should bring a friend along who can warn him or her when they are being taken. The Pisces may be a genius in the arts, but he is out of his element, usually, in the jungle of the marketplace.

With training, of course, any weakness can be overcome. But unless the Pisces is willing to undertake such self-training (practicality training) they are a sure bet to keep many a con man sleek, smiling, and in cigars.

The Gemini can be prone to frauds that take place in everyday situations, at the local shops rather than long-term investment deals.

An untrained Sagittarian, like the Pisces, is enamored with the concept of easy money. He tends to let down his guard when dealing with fraudulent people because of overoptimism. The Sagittarian is the type who will explain away annoying little facts and details with statements like, "why worry, it'll all work out in the end."

A person with a lot of Capricorn in his chart (Note: this means other planets in that sign in addition to the Sun. You can find this out by having your chart done.) will not make the native easy to defraud, but it will give tendencies to irrational fears about material security.

These fears will make the native susceptible to con men offering great "bargains," which the native may or may not need. The Capricorn may buy them simply because "it's a bargain."

This opens up another aspect in consumer fraud. Outright fraud and deception are not the only ways that consumers are victimized. There are many legitimate companies who manufacture finely wrought, quality items, who victimize the consumer by creating a *false need* for the product. This is especially true with luxury items. Through the use of lavish publicity and advertising, they actually create and stimulate desires for their products, which many families can ill afford.

This kind of victimization is much harder to deal with than outright fraud because of its subtlety. A false standard of living is foisted on the public mind. This false standard has little to do with a family's real necessities and legitimate priorities. So we witness the sorry spectacle of families who can hardly feed their members, but who own two or three cars, two or three TVs, electric can openers, a half dozen radios, and the latest most sophisticated stereo equipment, to mention just a few unnecessary luxuries.

These things are luxuries and they're nice to have—if you can afford them. But if you can't, there is no rationale for having them, or at least not for having so many of them. However, one feels a failure if he does not own these things and this is because of the clever, psychological techniques developed by some of the most talented and creative people in the country, advertisers. That such minds should be focused on such purposes is another sorry sickness of society.

Each sign has a different weakness in buying, and each sign is therefore vulnerable to the manipulation of a different false need. It would seem wise for each sign to be aware of his particular weakness so that he can resist getting caught up in it. What we are conscious of we have a chance of controlling; what we are not conscious of controls us.

Aries

The weakness of Aries, the pioneer, is his penchant for rash and impulsive action. This carries over in the area of buying, too. He's likely to buy too impulsively and on the spur of the moment, and thus is likely to make more mistakes and exercise poor judgment in his purchases.

Taurus

The weakness of stable Taurus is his often overwhelming urge for possessions. Though he is a very careful shopper and is cautious in going out on a limb, he is, nevertheless, almost at the complete mercy of the frantic buying mania whipped up by the media. His normal nature is basically materialistic; and when he sees all the new gadgets and items that come out everyday, he wants them all—whether or not he needs them. In fact, a Taurus will feel that he *needs* them all.

Gemini

The sign Gemini stands for everyday communication, commerce, and distribution. They have powerful innate urges to study, read, teach, and talk. They are not gullible people as a rule, and are protected from outright frauds by their strong logical mental natures. But they will buy many things they don't need or can't use. They are a sure bet to join many of the book clubs, ordering books that they may never read or will only read superficially. They will buy magazines and periodicals to excess. They are also likely to make their purchases from their close relatives who may, or may not, be shady characters. This is an area in which Gemini loses much of his vaunted logic.

Cancer

Emotionally sensitive Cancer, despite his protectiveness, is vulnerable to consumer fraud in products or services that deal with the home and family. When it comes to their homes and families, they lose all judgment and as a rule they go overboard. Tell them that a product will make their family healthier or happier, and there's a good chance that the Cancer will buy. They should be especially careful in hiring contractors, buying homesites, groceries, and appliances for the home.

Leo

The individualistic, creative, and fun-loving Leo has many weak points as a shopper. He has by nature a love for speculation, and this can cause him to gamble on purchases, and lose. He loves "the good life" and this will cause him to lay his hands on many more luxuries than he can afford. He loves to be the center of attraction so that he can display his kingly nature, but kingliness and sticking to a budget are mutually antagonistic concepts. He is notoriously vulnerable to sales pitches that appeal to his ego and that can cause him to be the victim of fraud. Leos have many virtues, but astute shopping is not one of them.

Virgo

When it comes to shopping, the Virgo is almost the exact opposite of Leo. They are careful, analytic, critical, and perfection-seeking shoppers. This makes them very difficult to defraud. They will carefully analyze every detail of a purchase and will detect the least little flaw in an item or business proposition.

The Virgo is very concerned with health, work, service, diet, and cleanliness. Quite often, they overemphasize these areas. This can make them vulnerable to phoney diets and remedies sold by quacks. They will also overspend on miracle cleaners that keep one's environment sanitary, spotless, and sterile.

Libra

Harmonious and artistic Libra has two weaknesses as a shopper. His refined nature makes him dislike any kind of physical toil—the kind in which your hands get dirty. When they are in situations in which these tasks must be done, they will buy every labor-saving device that they can lay their hands on, no matter what it does to their budget.

They are also, by nature, beauty loving. They are very apt to buy things just because they look nice and have a harmonious appearance, regardless of the functional qualities of the item. Given a choice between an item that works better and one that looks nicer, they will invariably buy the one that looks nicer. They also tend to overspend on "objets d'art," which is very noble, but is also very expensive. They also tend to overspend on clothes and furnishings.

Scorpio

Scorpio people are perhaps the best equipped of all the signs to resist "false-need" advertising. They are also the most difficult of the signs to cheat or defraud. If con men relied on Scorpio people for their business, they'd be in for a long, lean, and hungry winter.

Scorpio embodies within it tremendous powers of concentration and resistance. The sign stands for intensity, penetration, and the elimination of the nonessential. Natives of the sign understand how to do without if need be. And when they have a certain purpose in mind, they will completely eliminate all the nonessentials. Besides that they can spot a fraud almost instantly.

However, if the Scorpio has a certain goal in mind and certain products and services promise to help him achieve that goal, he may lapse into indiscretion. The Scorpio with an objective in mind is very one-pointed and may get blinded by this objective to be careless in some of the steps he takes to attain it.

Sagittarius

The restless and wandering Sagittarian is innately interested in expanding into as many experiences as he can. This makes him vulnerable as a shopper. He is likely to be defrauded or to make needless purchases in anything that promises to expand his mind, his social sphere, and his wealth. Sagittarians work by inspiration and direct perception, which is fine in many areas such as religion, philosophy, and the arts, but not too good in purchasing. In this area it is better to be more concrete.

The Sagittarian's love of travel will cause him to take numerous foreign trips, many of which he can't really afford. He should also be careful of the kind of travel agencies and hotels he deals with, some of them are notorious. When making a purchase, he should for the moment bridle his optimism and look at the thing objectively. As mentioned previously, optimism is often a prelude to fraud—overoptimism, that is.

Capricorn

These people, like the Scorpios, are almost impossible to defraud under normal circumstances. Like the Scorpio, the Capricorn is well able to do without and to ruthlessly cut away at nonessentials. Capricorns are disciplined, dutiful, careful, and cool. "Get rich quick schemes" mean nothing to them as they are willing to work long and hard for what they want. Their practicality, efficiency, and business ability is the most highly developed in the zodiac.

Yet, a Capricorn will stick to one product for the simple reason that "he's always used it." This may bar him from trying something new that is better and cheaper. His habits are very rigid and fixed in this area, but that doesn't mean that he's being defrauded. The product that he uses is sure to be good.

He is most vulnerable in his consciousness of duty. If a Capricorn can be convinced that making a certain purchase is a duty that he owes either to his family, career, public image, or friends, he will very likely make the purchase. In doing so, he may suspend his normal caution and care. He may make many unnecessary purchases, and he may even buy a shoddy service or product. He is also likely to make many donations to charities, institutions, and religious organizations out of a sense of duty, and some of them may be phoney.

Aquarius

The sign Aquarius stands for originality, group activity, science, technology, and anything that is new. The Aquarian native has strong innate compulsions for the new, the original, and the scientific. Their buying weakness is that this often leads them to purchase an item or service merely because it is new or different, or because it represents a new application of a scientific principle. They will go into debt, but they will have all the electronic gadgetry they can lay their hands on. Many of these, as mentioned, are quite unnecessary.

It is also interesting to note that the U.S.A. has its Moon in Aquarius. Never in history has any country brought so much technology and science to bear in the everyday things of life and the home. The commonest working man enjoys luxuries and gadgets in the home that a king didn't have even 100 years ago. Except perhaps for defense, most scientific research is in the area of consumer product development.

Pisces

As mentioned artistic and sympathetic Pisces is, as a rule, not a very good shopper. His sympathy, good will, and trust are virtues, but not in today's marketplace. When you indulge in commerce, good fellowship is important, but cool objectivity and discrimination are much more important. The Pisces is likely to make a purchase solely because the salesman happens to be a nice guy. He is also extremely susceptible to advertising which glamorizes a product out of all proportion to its function.

The Pisces tends to be impractical by nature and tends to buy things on whims and sudden impulses or for the lack of anything better to do. They will spend money on presents for friends that they can ill afford. They will buy the first thing that strikes their fancy at the first place they come to. Very rarely will you see a Pisces compare prices and products. What is most interesting here is that very often his strong intuition and psychic faculties will show him that he is being defrauded, but he will, nevertheless, go ahead with the purchase out of a misplaced sense of compassion and friendliness.

Advice to All the Signs

Any weakness can be corrected with training, but first you have to become aware that you have the weakness. Study the buying tendencies and weaknesses of your sign. When you catch yourself falling into it, when you are overwhelmed by a desire to purchase something that may either be fraudulent or completely unnecessary, STOP, check the impulse momentarily. Try to establish a temporary pause (a corticothalamic gap) between the impulse which is the result of a compulsion of your sign and the ensuing action.

Take a few deep breaths, yawn or stretch, but establish some kind of pause. This pause will allow the intellect and your other higher centers to come into the picture and aid in your decision. If this pause is not established and you act right out of impulse, the higher centers cannot come into play. You are then at the mercy of your subconscious which does nothing but react out of habits and compulsions from the past.

This is not *the* ultimate answer, but it is a help. The only answer is training and using our higher faculties that all of us have to a greater or lesser degree. If more people were trained in perception, fraud could not exist— it would be too easy to spot.

6

Astroguide to Better Communication

Nothing in the universe exists in isolation. To be is to be related. We can describe life as a structure of growing and dying relationships. Knowing how to set up right and proper relationships is one of the fundamental skills necessary to live a healthy, sane, and joyous life. In this area, the way a person communicates is vital. For, it is the communication between people that begins, maintains, and terminates any relationship, whether that relationship is of a social, love, business, or domestic nature.

Let's define communication as the *process* by which the *energy of meaning* is transmitted and received. Anyone who wants to improve his or her life, to make more of himself or of herself, would do well to start with improving his or her ability to transmit *meaning* to others. Those who really work at this will witness dramatic changes in their lives almost immediately.

Each of the twelve zodiacal types have different and

unique strengths and weaknesses in communicating. Whatever type you are, begin by recognizing your basic weakness and then eliminating it. This will allow your strengths to come out and work for you. Your communication and your relationships will improve dramatically.

If You Are An Aries

You are an action person. You like to communicate through deeds rather than words. Intellectual conversations bore you. So do discussions about abstract ideas, theories, and vague generalizations. When you talk to others, you'll be honest, open, and sincere. You're usually sure of what you say, and will express everything in a positive and affirmative manner. This is good. On the other hand, beware of coming across as too sure of yourself as this is often interpreted as dogmatism and is certain to turn certain types of people off.

You have a lot to learn about diplomacy and tact. This lack can spoil many communication attempts. You don't pull any punches when you talk, and will say exactly what you're feeling at the moment, regardless of the consequences. Be careful. This is often interpreted by others as insensitivity, and it's a definite block to good communication.

You're apt to get too aggressive and argumentative in your speech, as if you were fighting a battle instead of indulging in calm, relaxed conversation. And though you don't feel that you're being this way, others do. Slow down your speech, get calmer and cooler, and above all—listen more to the other person.

If You Are a Taurus

You're a quiet, easygoing person. You don't like too much talk, and have a tendency to be introverted and shy among people. You hesitate to get into verbal discussions because you feel that your mind isn't as brilliant as other people's. You also feel that you're not as glib in the verbal sense as the next person. Your mind, however, is fine. It works more methodically and slower than the average, perhaps, but it's also deeper and more thorough. As for verbal facility, you do tend to talk slowly and to be slow on the "uptake," but this is often a great advantage. You have time to think before you speak, a quality that's unfortunately lacking in most people.

Being a fixed sign, your communication problems center around an inability to see, absorb, and understand another's point of view, especially if it's outside your fixed mental-emotional framework. In a discussion you're almost impossible to sway, and can be incredibly stubborn. As a rule, you don't learn things through speech or mental communication, but must learn your lessons through direct experience—quite often bitter. Flexibility in communication is the main lesson you have to learn.

If You Are a Gemini

You're the communicator par excellence. You're an excellent student, teacher, lecturer, and writer—born salesman, too. You can talk to anybody, about anything, at anytime. You're glib, logical, cool, and matter of fact when you talk. Your mind is facile and quick, and your tongue matches it.

Your problems center around the fact that you talk too much and don't do enough listening. You've got to remember that communication is a two-way process, and listening is just as important—vital in fact—as talking.

When you talk beware of your tendency to jump from subject to subject and from idea to idea like some mental jackrabbit. This annoys many types—especially Earth signs. Watch your tendency to make snap judgements on what people say until you've heard ALL that they have to say. Try to enter deeply into what the other is saying, rather than just its superficial and obvious aspects. Much meaning always lies beneath the surface, and like a miner we often have to dig for it.

If You Are a Cancer

You're a warm, loving, and protective person—to those you love that is. Others can rot in hell for all you care—at least that's the impression you give. It takes strangers a long time to penetrate your hard exterior, and you don't make new friends easily. Once they're made, however, it's for life. Be careful of overdoing this attitude in your communication, as it makes many people nervous.

You tend to get much too emotional when you talk. You try to communicate your point by *feel* rather than by logic. Although this is effective when dealing with other Water signs (Scorpio and Pisces), it's annoying to most other types. You tend to confuse the *emotional force* and fervor put into a statement with the truth of the statement. And this is dangerous. The reverse is usually the case. The cooler and calmer the utterance of a statement, the more measured and rational it's likely to be. Get very cool when you talk, you'll get your point across better, and be better able to gauge the response of the other party.

Your sensitivity is very developed, and while this is normally a positive trait, you can overdo it. A person can say a harmless thing from his point of view, with absolutely no malicious intent behind it, and you'll take it as a personal affront. You immediately turn off to the person and block any further communicative rapports with him, and sometimes start an argument.

73

If You Are a Leo

You're proud, dramatic, flamboyant, and "kingly" in your communication. You're a lot of fun to talk to because you're warm, spontaneous, and dramatic. It's a kind of living theatre. You punctuate your speech with gestures and facial mannerisms, and there's always a lot of humor thrown in.

Like your brother Fire sign the Aries, you're absolutely sure of yourself and will make your points positively and affirmatively. Unlike the Aries, you don't like disagreement. You say what you say and everybody is immediately supposed to see the logic of it. You must learn that this isn't always the case. Sometimes you don't even bother to make conversation, you seem to issue "pronouncements and proclamations from on high." This attitude is fine if you're a boss telling your employees what to do, but it's very bad salesmanship and worse in social gatherings.

Begin to develop more sensitivity for the state and response of the other person. Be careful about unconsciously offending their sensibilities. Learn to listen more, and to be more aware of the points, valid or not, that the other is making. Don't always hog center stage either, walk to the wings every now and then and give someone else a chance.

If You Are a Virgo

You're quiet, modest, and shy among people. You seem to enjoy melting into the background. This stems from a root lack of self-confidence and a terrible tendency to overcriticize yourself and to be overly exacting on yourself. Axiom for all Virgos—you're a lot better than you think you are.

You have an excellent mind and can communicate very articulately when you feel like it. But you must realize that if *you* don't believe in what you say, others are not likely to either. It makes no difference how faultless your logic is, or how accurate your data, your point just won't ring true.

On the other hand, you may tend to turn your powerful analytical mind on the other people you're talking to, and this can cause major communication blocks, especially when it's overdone. Try not to be too exacting and picky about what people say. Before you criticize the details of the communication, try to get a good picture of the whole message.

If You Are a Libra

You're probably among the best communicators in your sphere. In social situations your abilities are unmatched. You know how to be friendly, harmonious, tactful, and diplomatic. You also have the verbal facility to get your message across clearly and logically.

Your communication abilities, your social graces, your genuine understanding of other people, and your harmonious disposition make you a born salesman and a boon for any public relations office. It also makes you quite popular socially. The only real communication problem you may have occurs when you bend over backwards to the opinions of others. You get too swayed by public opinion, and your point loses force. You must learn to put more trust in yourself and stick to your guns.

If You Are a Scorpio

You're an intense, serious, and determined person. Normal conversation bores you, and you tolerate it only when you have to. When you do engage in conversation, you'd much rather listen than talk. When confronted with the light, small talk that plays such a large part in many social gatherings, you tend to get annoyed. When you do talk, you make your point positively, crisply, and affirmatively, with a lot of emotional intensity and force behind it. The sheer force you put into your words, the zeal, and the fervor in your manner make you a very convincing, if not hypnotic, talker.

Your social popularity stems, not so much from social grace or witty conversation, but rather from the mysterious, magnetic quality that you exude. You do, however, enjoy meaningful talks. That is, conversations that deal with what you consider to be important matters—topics such as sex, birth, death, or occult mysteries. You don't like phoney people and will tend to show your displeasure openly.

You're much too serious when you talk, and should learn to develop a sense of humor. Be more tolerant in everyday communication; after all, in life we can't always be having meaningful talks. Watch that smoldering temper of yours, especially when someone says something really "off the wall." Learn to laugh it off.

If You Are a Sagittarius

You're very articulate, forceful, ebullient, jovial, honest, and sincere. This makes you quite popular socially, and an easy, pleasant person to talk to. You talk fast, openly and enthusiastically. When you get warmed up, you often get "inspired" and new insights come flooding into your mind—many of which you never knew before until that moment.

You enjoy talking about sports, travel, publishing, and literature. Your real love, however, is talk that concerns religion, philosophy, metaphysics, and the Higher Wisdom. You could talk on these subjects for hours on end, regardless of whether or not people are listening. Being a very positive type person, you could tend to lose sight of the other people around you and get swept away by your own enthusiasm and zest for what you say. This is dangerous, as too much of a good thing is as bad as too little.

It's also a good idea to slow down your speech and your verbal responses. Your mind moves quicker than most, and it's wise to give others a chance to catch up. Beware, too, of exaggerating too much. It's not that you do it deliberately, its just that you get swept up in the grandeur of your vision and ideas.

If You Are a Capricorn

Like the Scorpio, you're the type who keeps his cards close to his vest. You dislike talk—social or otherwise; you'd much rather listen. Light, meaningless, and unimportant conversations really annoy you. You're quite articulate and can communicate well and forcefully—when you feel like it. Most of the time you only feel like it when the communication concerns your job, future, public image, or social status.

You speak slowly, coolly, and cautiously. You choose every word, and you're always logical and to the point. This, of course, is a great asset, but it does have its drawbacks. It makes it difficult for you to show real warmth and feeling to those you talk to. Sometimes this is interpreted as snobbery or coldness. This kind of thing always hampers good communication, especially with sensitive types. Capricorns do attain great popularity socially, but it's something they have to work at—it doesn't come naturally to them the way it does to the Libra, for example.

If You Are An Aquarius

You're a born communicator in any area. You love to talk and to relate to people. Your friendly, idealistic, yet impersonal approach to others makes you a valued member of any group or organization. You are the born "friend."

You're articulate and logical with a gifted and wide mind that's always seeking new ideas and facts. You have the uncanny ability to be friendly and warm and yet can remain completely objective and detached when you talk. This is one of the greatest assets to good communication.

You have to be careful though, not to talk too much. Give the other person a chance to say something and really listen when he does. Being a fixed sign, you may have tendencies to be too rigid in your views. Once your mind is made up, it's very hard to change, and this can often block decent communication. Beware of being too unconventional and eccentric in your approach to people—at least certain types, anyway.

If You Are a Pisces

Your communication abilities depend almost completely on your moods. You're among the moodiest of people, and consequently a mystery to your associates as well as to yourself. When you feel like it, you're the warmest, most sympathetic, and understanding person around. You have the knack for saying and doing the right thing. You make people feel better when they're around you. At other times, you're completely out of it. People talk to you, but you hear nothing, see nothing, and respond in nonsequiturs. You're off in a world of your own and millions of light years away from the people you're supposedly talking to. Needless to say, this is a classic definition of a complete communications breakdown.

You're also much too affected by the emotional state of the person you're talking with. Strong emotions in the other person will tend to knock you "off center," and you lose your objectivity. You also have to learn to tolerate and talk to people with whom you're *not* in emotional rapport; that is, people you don't like and aren't in sympathy with. In life we meet all kinds of people, and we've got to deal with all of them competently and coolly or suffer the consequences. There's just no escaping.

Advice to All the Signs

It is obvious that communication is a two-way process. It involves both a speaker and a listener. When discussing communication problems, therefore, it's not enough to know your own strengths and weaknesses, but you must also be tuned in to the person you're talking to. You've got to try to understand the psychology of the other person so that you can present your communication in the most effective way possible.

Let's analyze the best way to communicate to each of the twelve Sun Sign types.

Aries

When communicating to an Aries type, be enthusiastic, forceful and positive in your approach. Speak bluntly and to the point. Try to avoid long-winded speeches as this will bore the Aries. Don't worry about being undiplomatic as this is not a trait that is generally valued too highly by this type. In fact, the more blunt and more undiplomatic your speech, the more endearing you become to the Aries, who will feel that he's talking to a brother.

Try to make your communication *active*. Emphasize your points with plenty of physical gestures and facial expressions. Try to *show* the Aries your point by making him experience what you say. If, for example, you're talking and explaining the merits of a particular wine, don't just talk about it—pour him a glass and let him taste it. In other words, try to communicate your meanings, as much as possible through *direct participation* on his part.

Taurus

When communicating to the Taurus type, speak slowly and calmly. Give him lots of time to digest what you say. Present your ideas in a logical sequence and don't meander from idea to idea. This is sure to irritate them.

Try to avoid ideas that are too abstract. Punctuate your speech with plenty of examples that are practical and down to earth. In social communication talk about money, possessions, real estate; keep your conversation on topics that are *substantial*.

Gemini

When communicating with the Gemini type, be witty, light, logical, and factual. Keep the tone of the conversation light and cool. Don't get emotional or too intense. With Geminians it is always wise to be a good listener as they love to talk. Let them, therefore, do most of the talking.

Let the conversation meander and roam where it will, and don't bother to keep too strongly to one topic no matter how important it may seem to you. A conversation that deals with just one topic is pure torture to the Gemini. In social conversation be sure you have plenty of odd but interesting facts, anecdotes, and news items to spice up the talk. Here, too, remember that the Gemini will consider you a good conversationalist and extremely smart if you are a good listener.

Cancer

When communicating with the Cancerian type, make sure that you take time to establish a sincere emotional

rapport. You can be the most brilliant conversationalist in the world, presenting the most unique and original information with brilliant and faultless logic—but if you fail to appeal to the Cancerian's emotions, your communication will not penetrate and your message will not come across. Show the Cancerian that you care about him or her as a person. Bathe them in warmth and good feeling, and then present your message.

In social conversation, talk about the home, your family, and the problems and satisfactions that are derived from both. Anything relating to these topics is sure to be of interest to the Cancerian type. If you are talking to Cancerians of the opposite sex, it's all right to get physical (holding hands, putting your arm around their shoulder, patting them on the back) if these physical actions are sincere expressions of feeling and concern.

Leo

When communicating with the Leo type, be enthusiastic and flamboyant. Try to make your statements positive and affirmative. In making a point try not to dispute or disagree with what he says, but rather agree and then reiterate your point. Accentuate the positive. The Leo has a strong ego and very often will not tolerate any kind of disagreement. Flatter him and appeal to his ego. Try to show that your message is consistent with all his beliefs. To illustrate your point, punctuate your talk with examples of what some celebrities and famous, prominent people have done.

Being a fixed sign, it takes longer for the Leo to absorb a piece of information than for most signs. It's also a lot harder to change their minds or opinions on things. Take this into account. Repeat a point often in various ways, using different language. This will ensure that your point really sinks in. In social conversation talk about the theatre, movies, gambling, and the city's night life. All of this is sure to interest him.

Virgo

When communicating with the Virgoan type, be cool, analytical, and logical. Don't get emotional, and don't display too much passion. Be prepared to answer questions and objections based on even the smallest details of your message—even though these details may seem unimportant to you. They're very important to the Virgo. Punctuate your talk with practical and concrete examples: examples that deal with efficiency in the home or at work.

The Virgo is a mental type and very practical. No matter what he may feel emotionally, he will accept a sound and logical presentation. In social conversation you can interest them by talking about health, diet, medicine, work and the technical details it involves, and service.

Libra

When communicating with the Libran type, be friendly and sociable, and present a pleasant appearance. Don't try to be too positive and affirmative, but make your point in a balanced way. The logic of your message is important, but more important is the beauty and symmetry with which it is presented. The tones of voice used, the beauty and rhythm of your language, the imagery of your metaphors—these are important to the Libra.

If you can present an argument to the Libran which is clear and logical and yet esthetically pleasing, your message will really come across well. In social conversation talk about love, human relationships, courtship, marriage, and the creative arts. These topics are sure to capture the imagination of the Libran type.

Scorpio

When communicating to the Scorpio type, be serious,
incisive, and direct. Speak to the point and avoid like the
plague, any irrelevancies. Be blunt and speak your mind.
The Scorpio is irritated by diplomatic pussyfooting, and
unfocused talk. Present your points strongly and positively, but don't overargue them, or try to convince them
by force. Adopt a take it or leave it attitude. "Here's what
I have to say, and these are my reasons for saying it—
take it or leave it."

The Scorpio likes plain and truthful talk, even if it
hurts. He won't respect anyone who is timid about speaking his mind. If your conversation isn't of a social nature,
don't try to become his best friend. In this situation you're
not looking for the Scorpio's love, just his respect. In social conversation be serious, but above all be sincere. The
Scorpio can't stand phoneys, and he's able to spot them a
mile away.

Sagittarius

When communicating to the Sagittarian type, be enthusiastic, jovial, and optimistic. Don't bore him with
petty details. Present the broad outlines of your message, and leave the rest to his imagination. To communicate properly to a Sagittarian you must stimulate his
vision and his desire to explore new mental and physical
vistas. It's all right in this instance to exaggerate a bit to
accomplish this aim.

As with the Gemini, let the conversation roam and
meander as it will. And you can bet that it will, but this
is normal for the Sagittarian. In social conversation talk
about religion, philosophy, metaphysics, travel, and business. All of these topics are fascinating to the Sagittarian.

Capricorn

When communicating to the Capricornian type, talk slowly, calmly, and coolly. Make sure that you are serious in your approach. Don't try to be the comedian with them. Present your arguments systematically and structuredly. Don't meander or wander. Be brief and to the point. Try to appeal to his sense of duty and tradition. Punctuate your talk with examples from practical business life that the Capricorn can relate to.

The Capricorn is organized and efficient and approves of such qualities in others. Try to make that kind of impression on him. In social conversation, talk about business, law, community affairs, social status, and ambitions. These topics and all their implications and ramifications have a special appeal to this type.

Aquarius

When communicating to the Aquarian type, be friendly yet cool and detached. Be impersonally personal. If you get too emotional or too personal, you'll make the Aquarian very uncomfortable. If your ideas are logical, it makes no difference how radical, unique, or new they are—the Aquarian will love them. Punctuate your conversation with examples and citations from the latest scientific and social theories in vogue. Aquarians love theories.

The Aquarian has a mathematical and scientific mind, and the more scientific your conversation is, the better your message will come across. In social conversation talk about groups, club activities, technology, science, and new inventions. These topics fascinate the Aquarian.

Pisces

When communicating to the Piscean type, be emotional, sympathetic, and sincere. Be friendly and strive to establish a deep personal relationship. Be idealistic and visionary in your approach. Punctuate your conversation with personal anecdotes and fanciful imagery. If you can stimulate the Piscean's sympathies—and this isn't too hard to do—your message and point are sure to sink in real deep.

Don't worry about sticking to logic and rational reasoning. The Pisces operates by laws that are extralogical. If you can get them personally interested in you, their intuition will pick up your point loud and clear. In social conversation, talk about music, poetry, ideals, mysticism, and topics of nostalgia.

7

Your Reading Habits and How to Improve Them

Man is a symbolic class of life. The ability to communicate meaning to another by the use of verbal or visual symbols is the prime characteristic that separates man from the animal. And though science is showing that animals do communicate with each other—animals can't *store* and *package* their symbols so that they can be communicated to their descendants, or to other animals who are not in their immediate space-time environment.

This ability to package experience and meaning into symbols, and then to store these symbols so that they are available to people who live in different spaces and times, has been called by Alfred Korzybski "the time-binding" principle in man. That one generation of humans can transmit its knowledge and experience to later generations in the form of books, records, films, and videotapes enables any future generation of humans to benefit from the accumulation of knowledge and experience of those who have preceded. Man is a "time-binder"; he doesn't have to start from scratch. He can begin where his predecessors left off. And it is this ability that enables man to *progress* from generation to generation and to build and improve on the legacy of his ancestors. Without this ability no civilization would be possible.

To illustrate this, try to imagine a world in which reading and writing does not exist. Imagine a Newton, a Faraday, or an Einstein making all kinds of wonderful discoveries that couldn't be written down and preserved for posterity. Imagine every young scientist in later generations having to laboriously rediscover for himself all the discoveries of Newton, Faraday, and Einstein. To do this from scratch required the entire lifetimes of three great geniuses, and in all probability would be beyond the powers of any one man. Progress would hardly be likely. Each generation would merely reproduce—if lucky—the discoveries of those who went before. Man might still be living in caves.

It's easy to see that until other and more perfect forms of communication are developed—telepathy, clairvoyance, direct perception, and so on—the skills of reading and writing are the greatest civilizing agents that humanity possesses. Inability, weakness, or wrong habits in reading cuts a person off from his cultural heritage and roots, and seriously limits his ability to acquire knowledge and facts about the world and himself. He is limited to only that knowledge acquired through his own personal experience and the experiences of those in his immediate environment. He has no access to the conclusions of the great minds that humanity has produced.

Reading, like all other human activities, is a function of the organism-as-a-whole. A person's reading habits, tastes, and hang-ups will be a reflection of what he or she is. It will reflect the person's psychological attitude to life. It is not surprising, therefore, to find that each of the twelve zodiacal types have a different approach to reading; each enjoys different types of literature, and places different values on the reading function. Each type also has different problems in reading.

Let's explore, briefly, the reading habits and hang-ups of the twelve astrological types.

Aries

As a rule the Arian type doesn't like to read; he'd much rather be out doing things. Ideas, theories, and abstract thoughts usually bore him. He's built for action and that's what he craves. If the Aries wants to improve and develop his reading skills, he should start off by reading a lot of action adventure novels. These will surely keep his interest and will serve to break the ice in his reading. Eventually, it will lead him to other types of reading which can be more useful in widening his mind and reaching his life goals.

Theory and action are two sides of a coin. To function well one needs a good balance of both. Just a theory without application and action gets one nowhere, so it happens when there is only action without theory. This the Aries must learn.

Even the Aries who is intellectually developed—and there are many of these—will more often tend to write or communicate his own ideas, rather than read the ideas of others. This too should be balanced off.

Taurus

Like the Aries, the Taurus isn't too fond of reading. Instead of reading he'd much rather be out working with his hands—fixing things around the house, watching TV, singing, building things. The Taurean likes to exercise his five physical senses. He likes to be involved in earthy things that are practical and useful. If he does read, it is usually "How-To" books, or books that deal with concrete subjects that a person is likely to need in everyday life.

The Taurus is a slow and plodding reader, but a very careful one. He'll chew and digest thoroughly, everything that he reads, and isn't a "skimmer" or a "scanner." If he does read anything that resembles abstract thought—and this is rare—he'll demand that the ideas and the whole subject matter be presented in an orderly, step-by-step way. No soaring on the wings of fanciful, speculative thought for him. And yet, this is precisely the type of thing that the Taurus needs to balance off. He needs to be exposed to a little abstract and imaginative speculation to get him out of his overearthly orientation.

Gemini

The Gemini is the reader par excellence. Everything and anything is grist for his mental mill. He'll read anything that he can get his hands on: novels, poetry, books on any subject, magazines, even advertising circulars.

The sign Gemini and the third house which it rules is associated with short-term communications and publications. Thus, we find that the Gemini is especially attracted to the reading (and writing, too) of newspapers, magazines and periodicals of short-term duration and view. I have known Geminians who avidly read the ads on the back of cereal boxes—they just love to read and learn.

This very love of reading causes the Geminian's problems in this area. They read too much and too uncoordinatedly. Their reading isn't organized or structured. Very often they become encyclopedias of unrelated and trivial facts, most of which are useless except for making of witty conversation.

Structurally, the Gemini cannot be limited to just one area of reading. This will soon bore him silly. But he should select a few areas that are somehow related and stick to them. This procedure will ensure that he gets a lot more out of his efforts.

Cancer

As a hobby, reading ranks low in the Cancerian's scale of values. He or she would much rather be fiddling around the home, playing with, or feeding, the kids, cooking, eating, and listening to music. The Cancerian woman will read cookbooks and "homemaking" magazines, and the Cancerian man will read books on home repair and improvement.

Cancerian types are fond of bringing back the past and reminiscing. When they do decide to read more widely, they're attracted to books dealing with the past, historical novels, factual history, biographies, and nostalgia. The Cancer will enjoy any book that can evoke strong and protective emotions in him or her, whether it be fiction or nonfiction. The old fashioned Gothic romance is a perennial favorite.

The Cancer, however, should try to read books that stimulate the mind rather than just the emotions. This will broaden his outlook on life and widen his mind. He needs to develop a more mental polarization to life, and reading can help him do it.

Leo

The Leo likes creative reading; books that tell stories and stimulate his own considerable creativity. He likes fiction dealing with the rich, the famous, the prominent, and the flamboyant. Tales of kings, princes, princesses, movie stars, entertainers, and "jet-setters" are his meat and drink.

Being a fixed sign, the Leo should beware of falling into rigid and inflexible reading habits; that is reading only a certain type of book. He should learn to widen his reading to embrace many subjects and styles of writing.

As readers they tend to be governed too much by their passionate likes and dislikes. If they like something, they like unreservedly and uncritically and vice-versa. Neither attitude is too good when it comes to reading, for here one needs to develop a critical attitude.

Virgo

The sign Virgo is ruled by the planet Mercury which governs the intellect and mental interests, in general. It is not surprising, therefore, to find that Virgoans are excellent readers with a wide variety of mental interests. They love to read.

They are analytical and critical readers. They're not the type, as so many people are, to believe a thing to be true merely because it is in print. The Virgo will dissect and analyze everything that comes into its mental sphere, and will only accept things if they are logical and accurate.

Their reading tastes run to technical manuals and "how-to" books in the businesses and professions. Whatever profession or field of endeavor the Virgo is involved with, you can be sure that it will be well versed in all the literature pertaining to it. Books such as on diet, nutrition, first-aid, and medicine are perennial favorites.

The Virgo's reading will tend to be limited to books that are practical in outlook and to those containing ideas that are concrete. Abstract ideas, mental speculation, and imaginative works tend to bore them. This could be a problem, since it tends to narrow a person's mental space. The Virgo should realize that the Abstract and the Concrete are two sides of a coin, and both are needed for proper mental development. Virgo should remember that everything that now exists *was once imagined*.

Libra

The Libran is a mental type but its reading will be oriented to pleasure and esthetic enjoyment. A book or novel does not have to be true or realistic in the factual sense, or useful or practical either. It must, however, be beautiful; it must evoke beauty in the reader.

Librans are prime believers in Art for Art's sake. Beauty is a way of life and almost a religion to them. When they read, they are not focusing on the ideas contained in the book, but rather in the beauty of its construction, and the art in the author's use of language.

The Libra loves books that deal with human relationships, whether fiction or nonfiction. The love story is a Libran standard. When the Libra finishes reading, it likes to feel an inner sense of harmony and contentment. Poorly or chaotically constructed plots, sad endings, and unrhythmic writing turn them off. One of the problems that Librans have in reading is their tendency to be lazy. They will stick to what is easy and esthetically pleasing rather than to what will do them the most good.

Scorpio

The Scorpio is a serious and intense person, and this reflects itself in his reading habits and tastes. Light, humorous, superficial books and articles dealing with topics of short-term interest are not for him. He looks at them as a lot of baloney. The Scorpio likes books that have deep meaning, that attempt to penetrate beneath the surface of these things and expose their inner essences and meanings—these are the types of books to which the Scorpio is addicted.

The only light reading that Scorpio indulges in includes murder mysteries, crime and detective stories, occult fiction, and action-sex adventures. One thing you can be sure of—the Scorpio takes deeply whatever he reads. He never forgets. Like the other fixed signs the Scorpio should beware of getting too caught up in rigid and fixed reading habits.

Sagittarius

The reading horizons of the Sagittarian are wide. It would be hard, indeed, to pinpoint any area in which they have *no* interest. This, in fact, is one of their problems. They can't focus for too long on any one subject. Sometimes they have trouble reading even one book from cover to cover. They get bored very easily. It's not that they're bored with knowledge itself, quite the opposite is true. They love it—all of it—and have trouble limiting themselves to just a few subjects when they know that there's Infinity to be explored. The Sagittarian must keep this tendency in reasonable check if he wants to get anywhere in his reading.

Sagittarians are turned on by books dealing with religion, metaphysics, philosophy, and visionary theories. They love books that deal with the long-term view of things, written by authors whose ideas are important to the future of all civilization. Books dealing with current and ephemeral fads bore them. Books that inspire one to live up to one's full potential, that widen one's vision, and that expand one's consciousness and perception of life are perennial favorites.

Capricorn

The Capricorn-type reader is essentially interested in books that help him build his public image, that help him become more efficient and organized, and that deal with his career. The Capricorn will carefully read any book that helps him toward his goals. He's a slow and cautious reader, but very thorough and deep. He carefully structures his reading habits and research to bring about the maximum results.

In fiction, his tastes run to deep and serious works. Stories in which the hero or heroine adhere to a stringent code of ethics, duty, and responsibility that are above and beyond the call of duty. Heroes and heroines who are practical idealists turn them on and excite their imaginations. These, by the way, were the types of heroes created by Rudyard Kipling and Jack London, both of them Capricorns.

Aquarius

To the Aquarian, reading (and writing, too) is as natural and important as breathing and eating. They need it to survive and to stay healthy. Aquarians are mental beings, and the scope of their minds is wide and powerful.

Their reading tends to center around the sciences, mathematics, and the occult. They like to read about the very ancient and the ultramodern, and it is customary for Aquarians to be immensely interested in ancient classical literature. It is safe to say, that if there were no Aquarian-type readers, then it would be difficult if not impossible for experimental and avante garde writers to find an audience.

If the Aquarian has a reading problem, it stems from too much not too little reading. They tend to get too caught up in their ideas and mental interests rather than participating in real life.

Pisces

Pisces is the sign of the creative imagination and fantasy. This is why there are many Pisceans who dislike reading. They would much rather be in their own colorful fantasy world than enter anyone else's. Very few writers have imaginations that are as vivid and "spaced out" as the Pisces type.

Those Pisceans who do read tend to like science fiction, fantasy, and romantic fiction. Poetry, too, is a Piscean favorite. They like any kind of reading which takes them out of the harsh realities of the mundane world and into other places. It is the Piscean-type reader who is most addicted to "escape literature."

The Piscean needs to broaden his reading to include more practical subjects so that he can learn to deal with everyday life more competently. This area is the perennial Pisces weak point.

8

Relaxation Guide for the Signs

"There is but one disease—tension." [Hans Selye M.D.]

The most revolutionary medical discovery of our day is that it is *stress* and not disease which kills us. It is stress which destroys the body's defenses against invading germs. It is stress which causes the heart, circulatory, and kidney diseases that now destroy more lives yearly than any of the other diseases. It is stress which causes premature old age and the diseases associated with the aged. It is stress which precipitates mental illness also.

From "The Mind In Healing" by Rolf Alexander, M.D.

That books on relaxation and antistressing have been on the best seller lists lately shows that the American people, at long last, are beginning to see the importance of the subject. It is about time. Besides being the cause of most diseases, stress and its companion, tension, also cause most financial, social, and creative failures that we see in life.

Weird? Strange? Impossible? Not really. Consider that to accomplish any goal requires a certain expenditure of energy. This is obvious. If I wanted to carry a hundred-pound boulder a distance of 30 feet, I must be able to produce 130-foot pounds of force to do it. Whether I generate this myself or by using a machine, such as a tractor or crane, makes no difference. That job requires the expenditure of a specific amount of force. Anything less will result in failure. Similarly with our personal goals, building a career, making money, or establishing decent relationships require the expenditure of time, toil, and intelligence. If for one reason or another we cannot produce the amount necessary, we fail.

Tension is one of the great wasters of life force that exists. To keep a muscle tense requires energy, and this energy could be better used elsewhere. Besides this, the muscular contractions tighten the arteries and veins that feed the area, thus forcing the heart to work harder to pump blood through. Again, we have a waste of energy.

Tension is caused by stress. Stress is caused by a variety of factors. Anytime the organism is required to do something, whether walking, talking, or thinking, certain organs and muscles are called into activity, thus producing some stress. This is normal stress, and by the way, this kind of stress is healthy for the organism. However, when we put too much activity on the organism for a prolonged period of time, we have a build-up of stress that becomes dangerous.

A person who works too hard, or thinks too much, or feels too much is putting extra stress on different areas of his organism. For stress is produced not only by physiological factors but by mental and emotional ones, as well. Thus health and sickness, success and failure, even life and death, as Rolf Alexander says, are directly related to how we think and feel about things. And learning to control our stress-producing moods—fear, anxiety, anger, and resentment—is essential to maintaining our health and happiness.

Living in an already overtense society in which everything is go-go-go and in which we are all more or less forced to live under a mechanical antinatural rhythm produces enough excess stress in most of us to cause serious problems. We need not add to this by indulging ourselves in negative thinking and feelings which only produce more stress and put nails in our coffins, prematurely.

Since we are all unique, each of us will become stress-prone by different things and for different reasons. What is stressful to an Aries will mean nothing to a Libra. What is stressful to a Virgo will mean nothing to a Pisces, and so forth. Thus, each of the signs must watch for different stress-producing moods in order to control them.

Aries

Since Arians are action people, stress can come from two areas. Physically, it can come from trying to do too much, that is, from too much activity. Emotionally, it can come when the Aries feels that his or her freedom of action is somehow limited or frustrated. This feeling can actually make an Aries a nervous wreck, especially if prolonged for a long period of time. With some Aries it is not surprising to find that no matter how much activity they indulge in, inside they feel as if they are not doing enough. They should be doing more, and the feeling of frustration comes sneaking in.

Arians must learn to measure their energies. They must learn to let go of activity after they have performed their daily quota. Life, after all, isn't all action. It is an alternation between action and rest. Trying to lead a life of only action is like trying to walk on only one foot. Imbalance is the result.

Taurus

Taureans are by nature conservative people with a strong practical outlook on life. There are two areas which are sure to produce extreme anxiety and stress in them: a feeling of financial insecurity and too much change in their lives and affairs. If Taureans do not have a certain amount of money in the bank at all times, if their creature comforts are limited, or if they feel that they are limited, Taureans will go into a panic. They just focus too much on material things and possessions.

If a Taurus is forced to change too much or too fast, this too will make him or her very panicky and stressful. They love the status quo. They love stability. This is all well and good, for stability is important in life, but it should not be taken too far. The Taurus must remember in such times that change is the only constant thing in the universe, and the only real stability in life is within change. And when things look bleak financially, let them realize that all of life is an alternation between lean and fat years, and lean periods will inevitably change if undertaken in a calm way.

Gemini

Because of their highly strung nervous systems, Geminians are naturally prone to stress as it is. The least little argument, or idea, or thought, or piece of gossip, or news item sets into motion a whole chain of neuromental reactions, opinions, thoughts, and speech. Their overactive brains, if not brought under the control, will make them extremely suspectible to brain fatigue and nervous exhaustion. From this they develop such maladies as insomnia, restlessness, and hyperactive nerve response.

For the Gemini, therefore, it is extremely important to

learn to turn off the mind and the thinking processes. They must understand that the mind is a machine like any other, and overuse will wear it out. When not solving problems, studying, reading, or planning, the Gemini should turn off his mind and rest it. He should learn to live more in the sensory world, the world of sights, sounds, smell, and touch, instead of the world of ideas.

Cancer

The Cancerian's feelings are sensitive enough as it is. But when they touch anything to do with the home, the family, and the children, this sensitivity grows in a geometric proportion. Any event that touches these areas, no matter how seemingly minor, Cancerians will magnify out of all proportion to the significance of the event. Thus, the family, the home and the children are the Cancerian's stress points.

To attain a more relaxed attitude to life, Cancer must learn to modify and deemphasize the focus of importance on the home. They must see that the home, though important, is not the only thing that exists in life. There are many other areas that are worthy of attention. They must get hobbies and crafts that they can retreat to when things seem to get difficult in the home. This deemphasis will help the Cancer see domestic difficulties in true perspective.

Another area that causes stress to the Cancer is their emotions. These are much too powerful and deep and usually out of the native's control. What is worse, they are usually identified with their emotions. Cancerians believe that they *are* their feelings, instead of seeing that they are beings, photons of light, functioning through many vehicles, of which only one is the emotions. The Cancer must learn (along with the other Water signs) that detachment is the beginning of control, whereas attachment to vagrant moods and feelings results in a life filled with stress, anxiety, and sickness.

Leo

Being, perhaps the most inherently creative of all the signs, Leo will get tense and anxiety ridden if not allowed to express his creative urges in some form or another. For the Leo the law is, "Create or Die." By death, we mean a long, slow, agonizing inner death that is pitiful to see. And this death begins with tension and stress. Being ruled by the Sun, the Leo must shine. It must ray forth its inner forces to the outer environment. Denied this, the Leo will become insecure and resentful, both of which are tension-producing states.

So shine on Leo. Get yourself as many healthy outlets as possible for your passion and enthusiasm. Dance, sing, act, go out on the town and party. Be good at what you do, and you will get all the recognition and attention you can possibly crave. But do not impose your will too heavily on others, which is a natural tendency, for this will cause tension and discomfort on other people and will rebound on you.

Virgo

In general, Virgoans become tense because of their overattention to detail. They get too fussy, too exacting. Everything must be perfect. I have seen a Virgo lady create a scene because her husband had a piece of lint on his suit, or because his tie wasn't centered properly. If one walks through life with this kind of attitude, life, being what it is, will be full of uncomfortable and stress-ridden incidents. This attention to detail is a magnificent habit when applied to one's creative life, or to technical tasks, but it is out of order in relationships with people and in the everyday mundane things of life. This Virgoans must learn. They must also realize that we live in a rela-

101

tive universe, absolute perfect does not and cannot exist. So, instead of searching for absolute perfection, content yourself with attaining a relative perfection which you can then improve on by degrees.

Libra

Have you ever watched Librans when they were in ugly surroundings, or when they were in the midst of argumentative and inharmonious people, or when they were forced to do tasks that are gross and unrefined? If you have, then you know what stresses the Libran type. Their artistic sense and appreciation contributes much to society, but the overrefinement which this brings tends to prove a vexation of the spirit when confronting the stark realities of this world. Yes, there is much ugliness, squalor, meanness, and grossness in the world, but somehow we must learn to live in it, to confront it, without losing calm and without sinking to the animal level. This is one of the main lessons of Libra. Beauty and ugliness, harmony and conflict are two sides of the same coin, and Libra must be able to handle both.

Scorpio

Scorpios, because of their intensity and passion, are by nature tense people. Although they seem calm on the outside, inside they are a raging torrent of emotional conflict kept in line only by the Scorpio's great will power. The Scorpio feels that he or she is always under pressure, and this, of course, reflects itself into their physical bodies.

Whatever the Scorpio does, it does wholeheartedly; it puts the force of its entire being behind it. The problem is that many of the ordinary tasks of life do not require all this expenditure of force and emotion. They can be done lightly and calmly, even humorously. This Scorpio must learn. Stop trying to kill a fly with a baseball bat. Measure your force to the nature of the task at hand, and take a more lighthearted attitude to 90 percent of what you do.

Sagittarius

The wondering, wandering, freedom-loving Sagittarian gets tense when forced to stay in one place for too long a time. When he feels that his freedom is restricted on any level, physical, emotional, or mental, then he develops stress and tension. If this goes on for any length of time, especially in a domestic or job situation, a fierce explosion is bound to occur.

However, this aimless roving usually has negative effects on the native's life goals. How can you get anything done when you cannot stick to a thing long enough to master it. So, very often, the Sagittarian feels caught between Scylla and Charybdis. Damned if he does and damned if he doesn't.

The way out for the Sagittarian is to allow himself or herself plenty of freedom but to put it under control—to set limits on it. Let the Sagittarian master one or two disciplines, or focus most of his energies on one or two goals, and then maintain many subsidiary goals that he can turn to when he feels bored. That the Sagittarian has places to turn when he feels bored or "fenced in" will keep him relaxed and happy.

Capricorn

Serious, sober, and self-disciplined, Capricorn is extremely distressed by disorder. Watch them. If they are in an environment of disorder and chaos, they will try and do something about it. If they can't, they get tense. In addition to this factor, there are many other things that make the Capricorn tense. Like the Scorpio they are more or less structured to be tense. They tend to overwork and drive themselves too hard. They tend to take things too seriously, and need to develop the lightness and humor which would melt away tension. They need to learn to work with an easy, natural-order rhythm. Everything in nature pulsates from action to rest, from go to stop, and this is essential for the Capricorn's well-being.

Aquarius

Aquarius, being the most mental of all the signs, has to be careful of living too much in the mind and not enough in the feelings and the physical body. Because of the pre-occupation with ideas and theories, there is sometimes a loss of contact with the emotions and body and the Aquarian will find himself in a state of tension without even knowing it. As with the Gemini, the Aquarian has to learn how to turn the mind off when he is not using it for any specific functional purpose.

There is another important area that can be extremely stress producing for the Aquarian. They have to follow tradition blindly. They are incapable of conforming to what the crowd is doing. If they are put into situations in which this is forced on them, they will get tense, anxious, and irritable, if not downright destructively rebellious.

Aquarians have to learn that we are organisms in an environment and that at times it is necessary to conform, as personally galling as it may feel. They have to learn the trick of discriminating between the times when conformity is indicated and the time when independence is appropriate.

Pisces

Emotionally sensitive Pisceans need a lot of mental and emotional space. If for some reason or other they are deprived of getting away from it all, going into seclusion and regenerating their energies, they will get tense and irritable. Pisces needs to dream—to exercise its creative imagination—the way other people need to breathe and eat. They need periods of aloneness to do this.

Too great an involvement in the practical affairs of life will also make a Pisces tense. But in this area they must really learn to discipline themselves so that they can handle everyday practical affairs calmly. If a thing has to be done, there is no use in emotionalizing about it, or resenting it, or fantasizing about other things, or as Pisceans are prone to do, escaping it. Do it calmly and well and get it over with.

The Pisces, like the Cancer, will often get tense if it cannot exercise its emotional sympathies. All that emotional power gets blocked up. It is wise, therefore, for the Pisces to exercise its emotions and release them through the arts, especially, music, dance, and poetry.

9

Sex and the Signs

If there is anything that contributes to the sexual hang-ups of the American people, it is definitely the incredible number of sex-educated books written, supposedly, to alleviate these very problems. When one considers that forests are shorn of trees to produce the reams of paper that go into the manufacture of these books, when one considers the huge amount of energy—both human and environmental—that is wasted in their production, and when one observes the negative effect these books have on the minds and well-being of the populace, then one can only conclude that our "sex experts" are propagating an ecological disaster of monumental proportions.

These so-called experts lay out rigid guidelines of what "normal" sexual performance and responses are. These guidelines, besides being ridiculously absolutistic, are usually based on

1. The private feelings of the authors
2. Inadequate observation
3. Quasiscientific procedures and studies
4. Ignorance of the cosmic process
5. Ignorance of the psychic structure of man

The much ballyhooed Master and Johnson studies are a typical example. Here they cloaked their ignorance beneath the respectable robes of "science," but what exactly did they study? They observed many couples making love under laboratory conditions. They observed the physiological changes that took place during and after the process. This was done by strapping all kinds of sophisticated electronic gadgetry; electrodes, microphones, and even cameras to the bodies and the sex organs of both parties. The results obtained were hailed as "scientific." In reality, what they studied was *abnormal and pathological sex*. No sane person would call the sex acts undergone in a laboratory where people were watching them closely, and with all kinds of artificial (and probably uncomfortable) electronic gadgetry protruding from their bodies, *normal sex*. The findings taken from such experiments must be invalid for normal, everyday sex situations. If anything, the Masters and Johnson studies are well-researched and documented cases of scientifically induced abnormal, pathological, and antinatural order sex behavior.

What is worse is that the researchers completely ignore the emotional-mental-spiritual context of the sexual act and focus only on the physical. As if the sex act were merely a function performed by two bodies—bodies divorced from minds, feelings, and souls.

What many scientists and so-called experts do not understand (although the more spiritually advanced ones do) is that analysis beyond a certain point becomes meaningless and deluding. As Isidore Friedman has said: "When you take a thing out of its context and study it in isolation, you very often destroy, in that very act of study, the essence and the meaning that the thing contains."

If one should chop off a human thumb and study it in isolation, using the best techniques and the best equipment in the universe, one would learn some surface facts about the thumb, but one could never learn the *meaning* of the thumb. One could never penetrate to its essence and real significance. For the thumb derives its real meaning from its relationship to the rest of the hand and to the rest of the body.

The famous story of the blind men and the elephant is a beautiful illustration of what happens when you look at only one aspect of a thing—when you analyze and do not synthesize (blend). One's conclusions are valid for only a very narrow and limited framework, and when seen from the larger context are completely wrong. Analysis without synthesis is ridiculous and worthless yet many of our experts are guilty of this.

What is the usual result of all these sex studies? People read them, and because they are written by "authorities," believe them automatically without further question. Then they either force themselves to live up to these arbitrary standards, and put unnecessary strain, anxiety, and fear on themselves and their partners, thus taking much of the joy and beauty out of the act or they may find that their sexual behavior does not always or consistently match the standards set by the "authorities"—*as indeed it cannot*—and they panic, become anxious, attribute all kinds of sexual maladies to themselves or their partners, break up otherwise beautiful relationships, and spend a lot of time and money visiting doctors and therapists. In believing that some arbitrary sexual standard applies to them specifically, sexual problems are created by a process of self-suggestion.

Alfred Korzybski, who formulated the science of general semantics, and who was one of the truly great geniuses of our time, always maintained that man was an organism-as-a-whole. No study of man nor of human

108

functions were valid unless they were approached from the standpoint of the whole organism, the organism in its entirety. All human functions, whether we are talking about eating, sleeping, walking, talking, reading, writing, making war, OR making love, are functions of the organism-as-a-whole.

A man can have the most powerful and most developed intellect in the world, but if he has an upset stomach, or if his body is ailing, or if he is in a negative and noisy environment, or if there is no heat in his house on a cold day, then his thinking will be very definitely affected and probably impaired. A gifted musician will not play up to par if he is ailing physically, mentally, or emotionally, or if he is forced to play in a negative environment. We have all heard how mental-emotional-physical problems can plague even the most well-trained athlete.

The human organism functions as a whole: as a unity. And *all* its functions will vary with the state of the entire organism, and with the type of environment in which it is placed. Sex is no different. It is a function of the *entire* organism, and its manifestations will vary infinitely with the changes in the mental-emotional-physical states of the people involved, the changes in the locale of the act, and the changes in the *time* when the sex act is taking place.

The implications of this are fascinating, and are borne out by experience. Can you, for example, equate the organism-as-a-whole response to a sex act between two people who really love each other performed on a secluded beach on a cool summer night, under a full moon and starlit sky, with the rhythms of a gentle sea whispering in the night, with a sex act between two people who just met at some singles bar (and who in all probability will never see each other again) performed in a sleazy motel room which has to be vacated in two hours? Absolutely not. The first would be a sublime, almost mystical experience far transcending the purely physical sensations involved. (Can you imagine trying to measure this type of experience in a scientific laboratory?) The second would be a pure physical trip done, most often, to satisfy an immediate sexual hunger. And although there is nothing wrong with this in the moral sense, it has no more meaning to the people involved than eating a pleasant meal to satisfy a hungry stomach. An appetite has been satisfied, and though this is important, the act holds no lasting significance.

Let us analyze this further. Sex itself is always an infinite variable. Two people can be very harmonious together sexually, but never will any two of their sex acts ever be the same. There will be highs and lows, peaks and valleys, in the intensities of their responses. These highs and lows will depend on the general energy level of each of the people, their moods, and the harmony of their physical surroundings. All of these are constantly changing. When a person is tired, tense, worried or depressed, not only will his/her sexual responses be off but also all his/her activities—thinking, digestion, and physical coordination, will be off. And most of the time all that they need to correct this is rest, relaxation, and a general change of mood.

In more scientific terms we can say that sex is a point-event in a space-time continuum, which will reflect the physical, emotional, and mental states of two persons at a given point in time at a specific point in space. If more of us understood this, we would stop worrying so much about our physical responses. We would stop being so uptight and tense about sex, *and start generating the proper mental-emotional and environmental conditions wherein, pleasant, relaxed, and loving sex could take place.*

Sometimes, of course, two people are simply inharmonious with each other—even though they both may be "normal" sexually. In this kind of situation the people either blame themselves or blame the other for what they think are failings. Rarely do they realize that neither is to blame. Neither was right nor wrong. Their physical-emotional-mental structures were simply incompatible and inharmonious. The proper exchange of energies, which is the prime function and characteristic of the sex act, could not take place. The people were vibrationally "out of tune," and no energy connection could be formed. You cannot, for example, expect the lights to go on in your home if the wires from the power station are cut or damaged. No power can flow because the structures necessary for it to flow do not exist. This is the kind of thing that exists in many cases of sexual (and, by the way, mental and emotional) conflicts. The thing to do in such a situation is not to blame anyone, not to run to doctors, not to read more sex education books, but rather to find another partner who is more structurally suitable to you.

Astrologers have long known that it is impossible to discuss general standards of sexual performance—or to talk about "the right and wrong modes of sexual response" in the abstract. It is not only meaningless but also downright destructive. For, like dietary needs, exercise needs, or clothing sizes, there are no right and wrong standards that can be set. The structure of each person is the sole guide in these areas, and so it is with sex.

The fact is that each of the zodiacal types makes love differently, has different sexual needs, and responds to it differently. What a Leo, for example, might consider a cold, frigid, and lackluster response to sex, Aquarian might consider to be the ultimate in passion and excitement. Neither would be right nor wrong, of course. They merely reflect the differences in their physical and psychic structures.

To repeat, sex is a function of the organism-as-a-whole. To know what is normal sexual behavior for you requires that you learn as much as you can about your personal and unique structure: physically, emotionally, and mentally. And here astrology can be a tremendous help. Having your chart done by a competent astrologer will teach you more about your unique and individual structure, and therefore help you more, than a thousand sex-education books, lectures, seminars, and medical examinations. Chances are that most of your sex anxieties are stemming from trying to live up to standards of performance and response which are not only arbitrary but also *alien* to your structure.

Generally speaking, the Fire signs (Aries, Leo, Sagittarius) will exhibit the most heat and raw passion in their sexual response, and as a rule they need a greater amount of it than the other elements do.

The Water signs (Cancer, Scorpio, Pisces) enjoy the emotional stimulation and rapport which they get through sex, the feeling of closeness and togetherness of sharing pleasure with another means more to them than the physical act itself.

The Earth and the Air signs are cooler and less passionate in their sexual responses relative to the other elements, and usually do not need as much of it as the others. The Earth signs (Taurus, Virgo, Capricorn) are stimulated by the physical sensations and pleasure involved in the sexual act. The Air signs (Gemini, Libra, Aquarius) love the mental communication that precedes and follows the sexual act. They are turned on by the union of two minds more than the union of the bodies.

Although, as we mentioned, the sexual responses and needs of every person are unique, people of the same zodiacal type (not necessarily of the same Sun Sign) will share similarities in their approach to sex.

Aries

The Aries will tend to be the aggressor in the act of love. They are as active sexually as they are in all things—and that, by the way, is *very* active. Their response is hot, fiery, and passionate. Being impulsive people generally, they tend to be impulsive in sex, very often jumping into the act without due preparation of their partner. They are easily turned on, and may or may not have too much use for foreplay and other preliminaries, depending on their mood.

112

Their sexual powers are strong, but they have little patience. Once into the act of love, they like to get on with it and get it over with. Afterplay and long periods of lingering in the bedroom bore them. Their lovemaking will be frequent, but more or less short-lived each time.

A negative or undeveloped Aries is likely to be selfish and egocentric in his/her lovemaking, quite often unable to see or understand the sexual and emotional needs of the other party.

Taurus

Taureans are very earthy people and sex plays a big part in their lives. Their lovemaking will be honest, unpretentious, and earthy. When Taureans indulge in sex, they indulge in sex, and that's all there is to it. One doesn't have to pretend to love them or idealize them in any way. Sex is sex to them, and it is good, regardless of the motives that underlie it.

Taureans will be slow and deliberate in their lovemaking. They need a longer turning on period than most zodiacal types and extensive foreplay is very important to them. Their responses are mostly physical, and it is the sensual pleasure of the act that they like the best—the seeing, tasting, feeling, and touching of each other.

They especially enjoy the sensation of the total possession of the loved one for as long as the act endures. Sometimes, of course, this feeling gets out of hand and they try to possess the partner all the time. And this can be quite irksome. A negative Taurus will have certain fixed and immutable lovemaking patterns. If this type has formed a habit of making love a certain way, in a certain position, for example, he/she will never change. They are, as a rule, not very inventive, original, or flexible in this area.

Gemini

Geminian sexual response is relatively cool and mental. Their attitude is usually curious, clinical, and matter-of-fact. One thing you can be sure of when making love to a Gemini: there will be plenty of talk. When this is not understood, many conflicts arise, especially if the other party is a Fire sign or a Scorpio type. Speech, conversational pleasantries, ideas and jokes seem irrelevant to these types when they make love, but it is ultraimportant to the Gemini. To turn Geminians on physically, you must stimulate their minds and more importantly stimulate their speech. Give them amusing conversation, and the rest will follow almost automatically.

Geminians have highly sensitive nervous systems. They tend to get tense and nervous very easily, and this can interfere with their sexual responses. It is very important, when making love to a Gemini, to get them to feel relaxed and comfortable.

Cancer

Cancer being a Water sign, is the emotional type of lover. They are turned on by warm, sincere, and intense feelings. Unlike the Geminians, the sex act to them is not merely the aftermath of a witty conversation, or a clever little escapade. It is an intensely emotional experience. They will rarely make love with a person unless they feel strongly attracted to them. It is rare for the true Cancerian type to indulge in casual sex with no emotional involvement. If they do, they are usually sorry about it.

The Cancer needs to be held, cuddled, and bathed in an ocean of warm feeling. Whether male or female, the Cancer will have a tender, solicitous, and almost motherly attitude to their lovers, before, during, and after the lovemaking. It is wise to go along with this as this heightens their sexual pleasure and intensifies their response.

Leo

The sign Leo has always been associated with powerful creativity. The sign contains an overabundance of raw vitality, spirit, and passion. And many astrologers claim that Leo symbolizes the orgasm, raw creative power in active and vital expression. It is not surprising, therefore, to find that Leos are perhaps the most oversexed of all the signs (Scorpios probably included).

As a structural fact, they need more sex than most people, especially when they have no access to creative outlets or hobbies. The sex act then, becomes their creative outlet—an area where they can express all their native passion, enthusiasm, and high spirits. It is a kind of merry game to them, not to be taken too seriously. If the other party is a sensitive type and does take it seriously, well, it is tough luck for them.

The negative, or undeveloped Leo, like the negative Aries, can tend to be too egocentric and selfish in its love-making. They just can't see, or perhaps they just choose to ignore the sexual needs, desires, and sensibilities of the other. They tend to feel that the world revolves around them and everyone else likes things the way they like them. The Leo is also aggressive and very quickly turned on.

Virgo

The sign Virgo represents the Celestial Virgin, and its cosmic function is purification. This is typical of Virgoan sexual response. They have a kind of prudish attitude toward it. Somehow or other they feel that it is unclean.

Their response and approach is almost diametrically opposed to the lusty approach of the Leo.

The Virgo is prim, proper, conventional, and cool in its lovemaking. It is something to be done and gotten over with, but definitely nothing to get excited about. It is not that they are bad lovers, far from it. In all likelihood they will have mastered all its technical aspects perfectly. It is just that they tend to be too unemotional and efficient about it. There's too much head and not enough heart and feelings.

Unlike the Leo who will spontaneously fall into a sexual encounter, the Virgo plans its lovemaking in advance.

Libra

If one understands Libran structure, making love to them is sure to be a beautiful and esthetically satisfying experience. For Librans approach sex the way they approach most things in life and that is from the standpoint of beauty. The Libran does more than just make love, it makes art, and this is an important distinction.

Libran sexual response will be heightened by beautiful and harmonious surroundings, by loving romantic pillow talk, by the sounds of beautiful music in the room, and by a skillfully contrived aura of romance. All of this is infinitely more important to the Libra than how many orgasms can be achieved in an hour or other sexual acrobatics. Sordid, hasty, and frenetic sex turns them right off. Before sex, take them out for a stroll in the moonlight, or to a concert, or to a candlelit dinner. These are the things that matter to a Libra.

Scorpio

Astrologers have long debated whether the sign Leo or the sign Scorpio is more sexually powerful. Leo may possess more raw sexual power, but Scorpio is definitely more intense and serious about it. Scorpios approach everything seriously, and sex is no different. Unlike the Libra, it does not care one whit about the aura of romance, or romantic settings, or cordial verbal pleasantries. When the Scorpio is into sex, it is into sex, and couldn't care less about all the irrelevancies and preliminaries. This intense approach tends to scare off or disturb natives of other signs who take sex more lightheartedly, and the Scorpio should learn to understand this.

Scorpios are passionate, emotional, and explosive lovers. They are easily turned on, long enduring, and do not like to let the act end. Being a fixed sign, their sexual habits can be conservative and rigid, and rarely are they experimental or inventive in this area. The Scorpio knows exactly what it wants and how it likes things, and that's all there is to it. Making love to a Scorpio is no game, it is very serious business, indeed.

Sagittarius

Unlike the Scorpio, the Sagittarian views the sexual act as merely one more sporting event in a long list of sporting events that it loves to indulge in. It is the "game of love," and as such, all its vistas, intricacies, and fine points must be explored. They are hot, passionate, and enthusiastic people, but unlike the Aries and the Leo, they need a lot of change and variety in their sex lives. One steady lover would soon bore the Sagittarian, unless that lover can supply it with enough variety and "newness."

Like all the Fire signs they are quickly turned on, and need a lot of sexual activity to stay healthy and not feel frustrated. Their sexual response will be heightened if there is a philosophical, religious, or idealistic framework behind the sexual union, that is if both parties are members of the same religious or idealistic movement, if both parties are working together for a "cause." Thus, the sexual union will take on idealistic overtones. It will also assure that there will be a lot of philosophical and visionary talk—something they love almost as much as sex.

Capricorn

It takes a long time for the Capricorn to understand itself sexually. They have a deep and innate need for security and safety. This often manifests in their sexual behavior. They need to feel secure and safe with their lovers if they are to respond properly. Very often this need manifests as sexual relationships with partners much older than themselves. This is especially true in youth.

They are also a naturally cool, taciturn, and cautious breed, and this too manifests in all areas of their lives including sex. I have had many Capricorn-type clients confide to me their fears of being frigid. They felt this way because it seemed to them (in their opinion) that it took them much too long to get turned on, and it also seemed to them that they never seemed to respond as heatedly and as ardently as their partners. What they didn't understand was that this was normal for them, and had nothing to do with frigidity or other sexual problems. The fact is that Capricorns need more time to warm up to their partners than most. This is the way they are structured, and anyone making love to a strong Capricorn type should understand this and keep it in mind.

The Capricorn is always unlikely to jump into bed with just anyone. Sex is serious business to them. And if they don't find a partner who meets their exciting standards, they are perfectly well able to wait until they do. They are self-controlled in and out of sex. They will be unselfish and capable lovers and very patient with their partners. You can also be sure that they have all the technical aspects of sex very well mastered. Whatever the Capricorn does, it likes to do well.

Aquarius

Like the Capricorn, the Aquarian is a cool customer, sexually. They dislike intense emotion and any undue display of passion. It goes against their grain and makes them feel jumpy and uncomfortable. They are the highest and most developed mental sign in the zodiac, and this is reflected in their approach to sex. It is mostly mental. They respond and react through their heads rather than from their feelings.

The Aquarian will have all kinds of theories about sex, and they generally love to talk about it and discuss it, but when it comes to the actual physical act, well, too much of it makes them uncomfortable. It gets too personal and they love and function best impersonally.

To heighten the Aquarian's sexual response, you must precede your sexual activities with a lot of talk, especially about high and abstract ideas, like science, philosophy, foreign affairs, politics, new life styles and ideas. If the Aquarian cannot relate to you on the mental, it will not relate to you well on the physical level either. But if you can stimulate them mentally, you will have gone a long way toward stimulating them, physically.

One of the problems that Aquarians have sexually is that they are full of theories about how it should or should not be. As mentioned, sex is an infinite variable and cannot be stuffed into any theory dungeon.

Pisces

To the Pisces sex can be an almost mystical and religious experience, or it can be just something he drifts into, either to satisfy someone else or because there's just nothing better to do at the moment. Their response will, of course, be very dependent on the emotional rapport

119

they have with their partner. They love the feeling of closeness and sharing that the sex act engenders and this excites them more than the physical act itself.

More than any other sign perhaps, the Pisces will indulge in sex out of feelings of sympathy for the other party. If they feel that by sharing sex with another that the other will benefit or be helped out of some rut, they will do it. And though this is very idealistic and kind, it does not make for passionate sex.

The Pisces is a moody lover and how it responds to a particular act will depend on its mood of the moment. One sure way to get the Pisces stimulated is to shroud yourself in an aura of glamour, fantasy, and mystery. They love that sort of thing. The Pisces is an incurable romantic idealist. By all means let the Pisces idealize you and put you on a pedestal, even when you know you do not merit such treatment. He needs it more than you.

The incredible psychic sensitivity of the Pisces makes it, very often, a sexual chameleon. It will reflect in itself the response of the other party. It can tend to lose its own individuality, and lose sight of the boundaries that exist between two people and to merge completely into the other. This has both positive and negative aspects. On the positive side, the Pisces will reflect and respond healthily to a partner who has a healthy and balanced approach to sex. Negatively, it will respond with anxiety and fear when the partner has a fearful and anxious approach. It is important, therefore, when making love to a Pisces to make sure that your emotional state is positive, and that environmental conditions are conducive to positive feelings and moods.

10

How to Say "No" Nicely

The other day one of my women clients was complaining to me. She said, "All you astrologers are really missing the boat. You all talk and write about how to attract, court, and make love to the different signs, but nobody ever talks about how to say no to the signs when they make advances."

After thinking about it for a while, I had to agree with her. Declining a sexual advance gracefully is a legitimate and long-ignored problem. Moreover, the problem is not limited only to women—not any more. Today, women are more open in the way they express their sexual desires and now men, too, are confronted with this often very sticky problem.

Of course, there are many situations in which you do not have to worry about being graceful or tactful about it. When you are dealing with a crazy person, or a streetcorner casanova, a bar room Romeo, or other strangers whom you will never meet again (if you can help it), you can afford to be rude and abrupt, as long as you get the results you want. It makes little difference how the situation is handled, since in these instances you are not overly concerned with the person's feelings or their future attitude toward you—nor should you be. These types, especially when they are rude or gross, should not be treated courteously.

But very often we are confronted with situations in which we *do* care about the person's feelings, and our future rapport and friendship with this person means something to us. How do you, for example, resist the romantic-sexual advances (unwanted that is) of your boss, friend, fellow employee, or best friend's wife or husband? You cannot be rude or hurtful, nor do you want to get involved. How then are these things handled?

In these cases it is obviously not enough to throw out a few stock, well-rehearsed, and memorized "brush off" phrases such as those many people use. Here you must have some understanding of the type of person you are dealing with. What is their psychological structure? What is the nature of their sensitivities and sensibilities? How is this person likely to react to a given mannerism or phrase or tone? In this area a knowledge of astrology can be most useful.

Dealing With An Aries

The Aries is a cardinal (active) Fire type, and when it wants something, it goes after it, full force and with no holds barred. If it likes you, its advances will be powerful, ardent, and immediate. Repulsing the advances of an Aries is not the easiest thing in the world. First, the advance is likely to happen so suddenly and quickly that you may not have time to "figure out what to do." Second, you run the risk of being swept off your feet by the sheer power and enthusiasm of its onslaught. The trick here is to keep your head and resist the initial advance smoothly and afterward there should be little problem. One thing about the Aries, it comes on like gangbusters at first and then it peters out. It is not too persistent as a rule.

When you refuse the advances of an Aries, be blunt, honest, and open. Do not be rude but do not mince words, either. Let him or her know immediately that you are not interested. Be direct and positive but do not be abusive. If you handle the refusal properly, you will have gained the Arian's respect, and your future relations will be friendly.

Dealing With a Taurus

The Taurus is a fixed (persistent) Earth type, and is inherently cautious and easygoing. It moves slowly in everything it does and is no different here. It may observe you for a long time before making an advance, but when it does more, you can be sure that it will be powerful and direct. The trick in refusing a Taurus is to spot its intentions while it is still in its observation stage BEFORE it makes its move. Once the move is made, you have a knotty problem on your hands, for the Taurean is nothing, if not persistent. When it finally goes after something, it does not know how to take no for an answer. This trait may prompt you to get angry or abrupt and then you run the real risk of hurting the Taurean's deep and very sensitive feelings. So be aware of its intentions before it makes any actual advances and discourage them. Show the Taurus in polite yet firm ways that you have no romantic interests in them.

Dealing With a Gemini

The Gemini is a mutable (versatile) Air sign and is quick, logical, and talkative. It will show sexual interest in people who are good conversationalists. It will also make its advances through speech and very casually and matter of factly. If you feel that your Gemini boss or fellow employee has his or her eye on you, minimize your conversations with them. It is probably impossible to completely eliminate all conversation with a Gemini, especially if you are in constant contact with them; but you can minimize it, and this will either turn them off, or show them that you are not interested in them. On the other hand, if the advance has already been made, you can divert the Gemini's interest by shifting the focus of the conversation to other things. If this is done properly, the Gemini will soon forget about sex and get into the flow of the talk. After that there should not be too much problem, as Geminis are not persistent.

Dealing With a Cancer

The Cancerian is a cardinal (active) Water type, and is ultraemotional and sensitive. Be extremely careful of how you repulse the advances of a Cancer type. Choose every word, and watch the tones of your voice. Watch your mannerisms and be careful not to betray the least signs of annoyance, anger, or disgust. At times, of course, this may be difficult, but you must try or else run the risk of creating long-term resentment and hurt in the Cancerian. Though they do not show it, their feelings and sensitivities run very deep, and they have long memories. When you refuse them, be warm and sympathetic about it. As you talk, hold the Cancer's hand or put your arm around his/her shoulder. Explain to the person that "you like him/her, but. . . ." Make it sound as if the reasons for your refusal lies with you and has nothing to do with the individual as a person.

Dealing With a Leo

The Leo is a fixed (persistent) Fire type and very powerful, passionate, and proud. It is a difficult type to "brush off." Their advances are very direct, ardent, and sudden, and they come on very strong. They are also quite persistent and have trouble taking no for an answer. Very often they will act as if they can not believe that anyone of the opposite sex is able to resist their charms, and when it happens, will feel that there must be something wrong with you for refusing them. Some of the negative type Leos think that they are God's gift to the opposite sex. It is a difficult situation to deal with. You can kid them and appeal to their egos with a line like, "What does someone as great as you want with l'l ole me?" If that does not work, say that you are afraid of the opposite sex or something like that. You will have to tell some convincing lie that will work the first time and yet not challenge the Leo's ego. But if this does not work, you then have two choices: you can give in or you can quit your job or otherwise end the relationship. If you refuse the strong-willed Leo, there is likely to be a long period of coolness and enmity.

Dealing With the Virgo

The Virgo is a mutable (versatile) Earth type, and is very cool, analytical, and practical. Unlike with the Leo, there is usually no problem in brushing off this type. They are very modest and unassuming people and plan every move that they make. If they feel no warmth or interest from the other party, there is little chance that they will come on and make advances. In the rare case that they do, just make up a logical (make absolutely sure it is) excuse like, "Gee, I can't right now, I've got the flu, and I don't want to give it to you." Anything to do with health or sickness will definitely impress the Virgo. If there are any problems with the Virgo, it is getting them to *make advances* when *you* are the one who is interested!

Dealing With the Libra

The Libra is a cardinal (active) Air type, and very gay, social, and harmonious. They are not pushy people and rarely come on too strong sexually or otherwise, to the point it would be a problem. They are very sensitive to, and concerned with, the feelings and opinions of others. If they sense that their advances are making you uncomfortable, there is little likelihood that they will persist. If you do have to repulse them, sexually, do it with diplomacy and tact. Say that you are in love with someone else and cannot divide your favors, or something in that vein. Love is something the Libra understands and can sympathize with.

On the other hand, the Libra is a very friendly person, and this friendliness is often misinterpreted as come-on. Do not make that mistake. Be sharp to discriminate between ultrafriendliness and a natural desire to please others, and romantic-sexual advances. If you do not, you will cause a lot of unnecessary embarrassment and seriously damage your future rapport.

Dealing With a Scorpio

The Scorpio is a fixed (persistent) Water type, and is very passionate, powerful, penetrating, and persistent. They are probably the most intense and concentrated types in the zodiac, and go after what they want with a kind of grim, relentless determination. With the negative types it is outright ruthlessness. They are a very difficult type to repulse because they are also magnetic and strong. In addition, they tend to remember forever every slight or hurt or rebuff. A negative type will nurse these, brood over them, and dream about revenge.

If a Scorpio type makes advances to you, tell him or her what you really feel—be brutally honest—they will spot a lie immediately. Honesty backed by strength of will is usually the best policy with Scorpios. Be prepared, however, to quit your job, terminate the relationship, or endure the wrath of the Scorpio. If you are lucky and the Scorpio is a positive type, you may gain its respect.

Dealing With the Sagittarius

The Sagittarius is a mutable (adjustable, versatile) Fire type, and they are very jovial, honest, and optimistic people. If they do come on to you, it will be in a good-natured and open way. There will be little nastiness or subterfuge in their approach. And, there should be little nastiness or subterfuge in your brush off. Match his or her jovialness and openness. If possible, appeal to their idealism. This will lessen any unpleasantness that may be engendered for the Sagittarian appreciates and respects above all else a person's ethics and ideals. Thus your excuse should sound something like, "It's against my philosophy, religion, or ethics to comply with your request, though I'd like to." This should be enough; for although the Sagittarian is not noted for taking hints, it is not very persistent.

Dealing With the Capricorn

Capricorn is a cardinal (active) Earth type and is serious, quiet, cautious and practical. The Capricorn is not likely to come on to you suddenly out of the blue. They tend to take their sweet time about things, and plan their actions meticulously and far in advance. Before they make sexual advances to anybody they will make sure that these advances are acceptable to the other party. On the rare occasions when they miscalculate, and their advances are not welcomed by you, take a serious and sober approach. Explain that you think that this affair would either hamper your efficiency, or interfere with your duties and responsibilities which lie elsewhere. This type of rebuff, if done right, will not only take you off the hook but also will gain the Capricorn's respect. Duty and responsibility are the twin virtues that he loves the most.

Dealing With An Aquarian

The Aquarius is of the fixed (persistent) Air category, and they are mental, friendly, and unconventional. In fact, you never know when or why they decide to do anything, much less make an advance. If their advances bother you, the best thing to do is to engage them in unconventional and "spaced out" conversation. Get them "stoned" on ideas and theories and chances are they will forget all about coming on to you and get lost in the conversation.

There is danger in this approach, however, for if you succeed too well in making interesting and original conversation, the whole thing could backfire. The Aquarian may get so fascinated that it may fall head over heels in love! Then the complications really begin! The Aquarian can be most persistent and self-willed when it wants something. If all else fails, tell him/her, quietly and calmly that you love him/her as a friend, even as a brother or sister. They will understand that and may even like it. The Aquarian is the born friend and they love to be put in that role.

Dealing With the Pisces

The Pisces is a mutable (versatile) Water type, and is extremely moody, dreamy, and sympathetic. Whether or not the Pisces makes an advance toward you will depend on its mood of the moment. In one type of mood the Pisces might not even know that you exist, and in another it may be all over you confessing its love. Repulsing Pisces is not too hard as long as you are careful not to hurt their ultrasensitive feelings. Whatever explanation you give, provided it is not malicious or nasty, and provided it is *sincere* will go over with the Pisces. They are not very persistent and are not very likely to bother you again. They will understand your position, probably sympathize with it, and forgive you.

11

Planning Your Astrovacation

Planning a vacation these days can be a delight or a disaster. There is just so much to choose from. Should one go on a cruise, fly to Europe, swing in Vegas, lounge around at some oceanside resort, go on a camping trip, visit Uncle Moe in Oshkosh, or just drive cross country? No matter what you decide to do, you get the nagging feeling that you are missing out on something and that you have made the wrong choice.

A knowledge of astrology, besides the many other boons it bestows, can help us in this area. For real astrology is the most practical of sciences. You can use it with profit in almost all areas of your life-activities, whether making a really important decision like marriage or business partnership, or a relatively unimportant decision like choosing the best clothes to wear, or planning your vacation.

We all do things differently. We enjoy different activities, different friends and associates, and function best in different environments. These differences have their roots in the inherent differences in our psychological make-ups. To enjoy any activity to its fullest, we should not only understand the nature of the activity but also we should have a sharp knowledge of our own personal structure, and then weigh the activity against it. Vacationing is, of course, no different. Its main purpose seems to be to provide a change, an alternation of activity, which is so necessary for psychic and physical health.

In these times, when most of us are subjected to many unnatural stresses and strains which come from living in a technocracy, stresses and strains, which perhaps no other generation has ever had to endure; when most of us are forced to do work which we inherently do not like, vacationing takes on real importance. It is important not so much for the so-called rest we get—very few people really get any rest on vacation—but because of the *change* it provides. For a certain period during the year we have the relative freedom to do what we like.

Since each of the signs likes to do different things, it is not surprising that each will have different preferences in vacations. Let us explore these briefly.

Aries

Aries is a cardinal, Fire sign and its keyphrase is I AM. It is the pioneer of the zodiac, and its motto is action. The best vacation for an Aries, therefore, would be in a place or locale which gives it the utmost freedom of action. As a rule, it can not tolerate traditional resorts, or cruise ships where most of the activities are limited to the physical locale of the ship or resort. This goes double for those prepackaged group tours, where the activities are planned and highly structured. The Aries cannot stand the rigid dress regulations and the codified meal hours that exist in most resorts, ships, and tours.

The best type of vacation for the Aries is either a

camping trip where it is free to roam where and how it wants, eat when and what it feels like and where it does not have to answer to anybody for its behavior, or a resort that promises the same thing. The resort should be big enough so that the Aries does not feel cramped, and it should have enough facilities to satisfy the Arian's need for physical activity.

Taurus

Taurus is a fixed, Earth sign and its keyphrase is I POSSESS. It loves stability, leisure, and material and physical substance. Whereas, the Aries does not really care about its physical surroundings as long as it has its freedom of action, the Taurean feels exactly the reverse. At home, at the job, or on vacation, it wants its physical comforts. It wants to be surrounded by beautiful things and feel that for the time of its vacation, it is master of all that it surveys.

It loves opulent and lavish resorts, especially those that are located in rural, farm, or mountain areas. They love to be near the earth and surrounded by the smells of good growing things. They love the rigid scheduling of the traditional resort where all the meals are served at fixed times, where all the activities are preprogrammed in a fixed schedule, and where the patterns of behavior of guests and management are conservative. The resort must serve plenty of good food. With these ingredients the Taurean is sure to have a delightfully satisfying vacation.

Gemini

Gemini is a mutable, Air sign and its keyphrase is I THINK. They love to talk, learn, and be in places where there is plenty of change, and plenty of conversation.

The third house which Gemini rules deals with short

journeys, and this is usually the type of vacation that the Geminian likes. As a rule they do not go in for long distances or foreign travel but prefer to spend their time near their neighborhood, or in environments and resorts that simulate neighborhood conditions. They also like to spend their vacations at or near the homes of their close relatives (also ruled by the third house). The Gemini is apt to regard its vacation time as a perfect opportunity to visit and to cement relationships.

Another type of vacation that is ideally suited for the Gemini is that of going to some resort to take courses. Here, they combine learning with fun at a resort atmosphere.

Cancer

Cancer is a cardinal, Water sign and its keyphrase is I FEEL. They love their homes and are sensitive to outside environments. Like the Gemini, the Cancer does not like long distance or foreign travel. It is customary for them to spend their vacations at home with their families, rather than going anywhere special. When they do go away, they prefer resorts or areas that have a family-type atmosphere, where people come with their kids and where there are good daycamps for them; and preferably a resort that is family-owned and operated by a family who treat the guests warmly and personally. Cancerians should avoid those big, gaudy, factory-type resorts where the guests are treated impersonally, by the numbers. Although these resorts invariably boast having almost any facility and activity that one can imagine, the cold atmosphere will definitely make the Cancer feel out of place and uncomfortable. Another type of vacation that the Cancer enjoys is renting a bungalow or cottage near the sea and running its own household the way it sees fit.

Leo

The Leo is a fixed, Fire sign and its keyphrase is I WILL. They are a proud, fun-loving and flamboyant breed. They love the good life and enjoy environments that are lavish, opulent, and gaudy. The bigger and brasher the place, the better they like it. There should be a lot of people and a lot of excitement, and most important, there should be opportunities for the Leo to "king it."

They need an active night life and revel in lavish entertainment spectaculars. They love the rituals of dressing up, dancing, and letting loose. This is all high drama to the Leo, and there is nothing the Leo likes better than drama, preferably with itself in the center stage. The resort or vacation that they choose should be able to supply them with all of these.

The Leo also has a strong penchant for gambling, and this makes them particularly attracted to resort areas like Las Vegas, Monte Carlo, and Paradise Island. These places seem to combine pomp, pageantry, luxury, night-life, and gambling all rolled into one. A kind of Leo heaven.

Virgo

Virgo is a mutable, Earth sign and its keyphrase is I ANALYZE. They are down to earth, practical, and mentally alert people. Virgoans as a rule like to keep busy, and it is often hard to get them to take any vacation at all. Virgoans have to be urged to rest and relax as there is a real danger of them overworking themselves. However, since they are especially interested in their health, if you can make them see that a vacation is needed for health reasons, they will go. A health spa, by the way, is an ideal Virgoan retreat. The diets are planned scientifically and so are the activities.

They also like quiet little places in the woods or mountains which are close to nature. If they stay at a traditional resort, they should make absolutely sure that the service and sanitary conditions are up to their high standards. Perhaps they should visit the place before they register or inquire about it from friends, preferably other Virgoans. There is nothing that will turn a Virgo off more than being forced to stay at a place where the lobbies, kitchens, dishes, and rooms are not spotless.

Libra

The Libra is a cardinal, Air type and its keyphrase is I BALANCE. They are harmonious, social-minded and beauty-loving people. The vacation they choose should reflect this. A vacation at an art or writers colony would be ideal. They also enjoy resorts featuring strong art programs and good entertainment. The resort they choose should attract a more refined crowd, and there should be plenty of opportunities for socializing and love. The resort should be beautiful but not garish or gaudy, and its location should be scenic. The atmosphere should be a kind of subdued formality. Like the Leo, the Libra likes to dress up and go out, but it finds the Leo's ostentation distasteful.

Scorpio

Scorpio is a fixed, Water sign and its keyphrase is I DESIRE. They are intense, introverted, and basically secretive people. As a rule they do not like crowds, and they do not enjoy the small social chit-chat that is prevalent in most big resorts. The Scorpio much prefers to be alone or to be with one or a few others whom it likes and respects. A small cabin near a lake, a bungalow near the ocean, a cruise on a relatively small ship, a flight to a relatively hidden and secluded part of the world are the types of vacations Scorpio enjoys. The single Scorpio will often go to crowded resorts to meet other singles, but when it meets what it wants, which does not take too long, it disappears from sight with its partner.

Sagittarius

Sagittarius is a mutable, Fire sign and its keyphrase is I SEE. They are jovial, convivial, and fun-loving people. If it were up to them their whole lives would be one big vacation, and they would spend it traveling around from one foreign country to another. Travel is their meat and drink, and this is what you will find them doing on their vacations. If the Sagittarian person is stuck at a desk job all year round, this type of vacation is an absolute necessity. But if the Sagittarian is holding a job that demands a lot of travel, and this is very often the case, then perhaps a better change of pace would be sticking to some local resort. It is a nice change, and if the resort allows them a lot of physical activity, especially sports and horseback riding, they should have a lot of fun.

Capricorn

Capricorn is a cardinal, Earth sign and its keyphrase is I USE. They are serious, practical, organized, and secretive people. Frivolity and superficiality bore them silly. They will avoid at all costs environments where they have to deal with people like that, unless, of course, it is in the line of duty. In the line of duty, the Capricorn will submit to almost anything. The Capricorn enjoys being alone and close to nature. Camping trips to the mountains and other secluded areas really recharge them. They especially like mountain climbing.

On the other hand, you will often find them at resorts, spas, and cruises where prominent and important people go. The tenth house ruled by Capricorn, is associated with one's career and image before the public. If a particular resort, or vacation will foster that image, the Capricorn is likely to be there.

Aquarius

The Aquarius is a fixed, Air sign and its keyphrase is I KNOW. They are original, freedom-loving and ultra-individualistic people. They get much pleasure out of showing their individuality through association with groups. Any vacation they take will have to afford them plenty of opportunity to socialize with people. They are also usually fond of group and organizational tours, most of these they themselves have probably helped to organize. They love international travel, but will be attracted to any resort or tour that is unique, bohemian, and unconventional. They will also be attracted to resorts that are ultra-modern in decor and facilities.

Pisces

Pisces is a mutable, Water sign and its keyphrase is I BELIEVE. They are a sensitive and impressionable breed, and environments and people affect them very deeply, more deeply perhaps than any other sign of the zodiac. The Pisces, therefore, should be especially careful in planning its vacation. Unfortunately, however, they are the least likely of any of the signs to plan anything, much less a vacation. They are very likely to go off anywhere at the spur of the moment, and let their intuition guide them, or they let their friends lead them to a place.

The Pisces loves, in fact, needs to be around water.

Any resort, spa, cruise, or cabin that brings them near water will definitely attract them. Pisceans are moody people, and depending on their mood of the moment, they will either want to socialize or be alone and dream. They need a resort that can offer them both.

12

Selling the Signs: An Astrological Guide for Salesmen

There are many ways to describe any given item. If your job is selling that item, you had better be familiar with them all. Millions, perhaps billions, of dollars have been spent by market researchers and analysts in studying the motivations behind buying. All the studies seem to point to one basic result. A person buys an item to fill a certain need. However, since everyone is different each has different needs. The job of the salesman is to match his salespitch to the need of the particular person he is confronting. This ability is what distinguishes the talented salesman from the hack.

To those who sell for a living this is perfectly obvious. To those who do not sell, here are some explanations. Have you ever noticed the variety of ways that automobiles are advertised and sold? Check on it sometime, you will be amazed. Now a car is basically a machine that provides (hopefully) safe, efficient, and comfortable transportation. All cars have this in common. Yet, there are hundreds of makes and models, each of which is designed to meet the needs of a certain group of buyers. Moreover, each make and model is sold and presented differently. Small car manufacturers stress the economy angle; big car manufacturers stress roominess and comfort; sports car manufacturers stress performance and speed; luxury car manufacturers use the snob appeal by appealing to the buyer's ego.

This variety of approach is not limited to different makes and models. Very often the same make is presented differently. We have all seen this many times. One ad will stress the sex angle, another will stress beauty, and some ads do not even stress the product at all: they will merely present some humorous or entertaining scene, and just mention the product in passing.

The point is that *all* these approaches work. And the reason they work is that different people are "turned on" by different things. And although businessmen have discovered this relatively recently, astrologers have known this for millennia. This principle is, in fact, at the heart of all astrological theory and practice.

Astrology can be an enormous help to a salesman. If you have a little insight into the character of the person you are dealing with, you can automatically adjust your sales angle accordingly. This does not mean that you misrepresent the product or indulge in any kind of falsehood. All it means is that you have some kind of a guide, a map, for selecting and using out of a vast array of possible descriptions and presentations, an angle of approach best suited to appeal to the particular prospect you are confronting. And although astrological knowledge can be misused in this area, it is not wise to do so. The structure of the Cosmic Process is such that whatever we do, whether good or ill, *must* come back to us.

This information, while aimed at the professional salesman, should be useful to anybody: the wife who wants her husband to buy a new dishwasher, the secretary who wants a new typewriter, the son who wants a car, or the executive who wants to sell the higher ups on an idea. In life, at one time or another, all of us are called on to sell something; it could be an idea, a product, or oneself.

Generally speaking, you would sell the Fire signs (Aries, Leo, Sagittarius) by appealing to their egos, their sense of self. And the more zeal, gusto, and enthusiasm you can inject into your presentation the better.

With the Water signs (Cancer, Scorpio, Pisces) you would appeal to their feelings and sympathies. With these signs the product is often secondary and your best bet is to sell yourself. You must establish an emotional rapport.

With the Air signs (Gemini, Libra, Aquarius) your appeal is to the intellect. You must be cool, detached, and logical. Your presentation should be flexible and free-wheeling with a lot of ideas.

With the Earth signs (Taurus, Virgo, Capricorn) your appeal is to their practical sense. Your approach is sober, conservative, and very businesslike. Your presentation should be limited strictly to the concrete uses and economic factors of your product.

To Sell An Aries

These people are primarily interested in action—especially an action that calls for starting something new. They are the doers and the pioneers of the zodiac. Your presentation should stress all the new projects the customer will be able to start if he buys the product. Go into great detail on this point. Hammer away at it. Excite his will to do. Do not bother too much about things like durability, cost analyses, or financing. When the Aries sees new vistas of action, he tends to ignore or pay the scantiest of attention to these "details." If you persist in discussing details when not asked, you run the grave risk of boring him. With an Aries you must be very careful about that because they bore easily and are apt to get impatient. Above

141

all keep your presentation focused on the *immediate* benefits of your product or idea. You will never sell an Aries by talking about long-term considerations.

To Sell a Taurus

Taureans have a tremendous drive for material stability. They love to buy and own things. However, they are very careful shoppers and demand substance and durability in what they buy. This is the point you must stress. Talk about the solidity and durability of your item; tell him how many years it will last; tell him how it will help stabilize his home or business. Keep the talk focused on the product, do not go off on a tangent.

Taureans are very sense oriented. Their view of the world is shaped, not so much by ideas, but by sensory impressions. If possible, bring a sample of your product with you, something the customer can see and touch. If this is impossible, describe your product vividly; describe what it looks like, what it feels like, smells like, and tastes like. If you can stimulate his senses, nine times out of ten you will get a sale. One more thing. Dress and act very conservatively. Taureans, as a rule dislike anything too "far out" or extreme.

To Sell a Gemini

This is a mental sign. These people love to talk, to study, and to learn new things. The Gemini loves to collect facts. Do not get emotional or too enthusiastic as this tends to embarrass them. Instead establish a nice, easy, light, and cool conversation. Talk about anything and everything, but throw in a lot of facts and tidbits of information. Talk about the kind of trip you had getting to his place; the weather; the score of last night's ballgame; the latest book you read; tell him some funny stories. Once you have done this you can begin your sales talk. Be flexible and expect a lot of questions, interruptions, and even changes of topic. These people have a lot on their minds and are always eager to learn more. A stiff, rigid, and formal presentation is a sure way to turn them off. In describing your product, stress its versatility and adaptability. Show all the different and various things it is capable of. Go into great detail here.

Above all, don't get flustered if you wind up doing more listening than talking; this is part of the game. For with these people your powers of communication will be tested to the utmost, and good communication implies being as good a listener as you are a talker.

To Sell a Cancer

Be careful when selling these people. They are moody and ultrasensitive. This sensitiveness has a tendency to become defensiveness, and you never know what may trigger it off. Tread lightly and watch every word; watch especially the tones of your voice.

When you approach a Cancerian try to see what kind of mood he is in. If it is a bad one, try to reschedule your appointment for some other time. In these cases there is little point in even trying to get friendly. If, however, his mood is stable, begin immediately to try to establish an emotional rapport. Put genuine *feeling* into what you say. Really feel inside that your product is good and useful, and that it is the best in the world. Do not even attempt this if you cannot be sincere. The Cancerian will spot a phoney emotion immediately.

The soft sell is your best bet; the super high-powered approach is more likely to put a Cancerian off and drive him deeper into his shell. Be soft, warm, and soothing. If possible, take him out to lunch and discuss your business there. The more personal and less businesslike you can make your approach the better.

In your presentation try to bring out (if at all possible)
that the use of your product or idea will somehow (1)
make home life more satisfying and enjoyable, directly
or indirectly; and (2) assist him in nourishing and protecting those he loves, directly or indirectly. If he is a
regular customer appeal to his loyalty, either to you or
to your company.

To Sell a Leo

These people are proud and extremely individualistic.
They genuinely enjoy the good things in life. Like the
Taurean the Leo likes to buy, but not for the same reasons. Whereas the Taurean enjoys the sense of ownership,
the Leo buys for the sheer enjoyment of the product.

Your presentation should be geared to the Leo's ego,
for here more than with any other sign, the snob appeal is
most effective. Show him how the ownership of your item
will make him unique, or make him a leader, or build his
reputation, or make him the envy of all his fellows, or
make him a trendsetter. Tell him that your item is designed to appeal to only an ultraselect group of people,
of which he is one. Above all talk about the pleasures and
the fun to be had as a result of using your product or
idea.

There is no need to worry about the price or financing.
If he likes your product, this issue will not be a factor.
Leos are notoriously extravagant and tend to buy now and
worry about prices later.

To Sell a Virgo

Virgoans are the best technicians and analysts in the
zodiac. Their strong eye for detail can tend to make them
critical. It is, therefore, wise to dress clean and neat,
shave close, and have all your facts and data well re-

hearsed and very clear in your mind. Remember, you are dealing with someone who notices *everything* and who is most probably going to be analyzing and scrutinizing everything you say and do—be prepared!

Make sure your presentation is logical, cogent, and well organized. Discuss every aspect of the product; analyze it in great detail and with clarity. Omit nothing. Take nothing for granted.

Stress the practical service that the product will give; stress the details it can handle or eliminate; talk about the warranty and service and maintenance contracts your company offers; try to bring in the health angle, showing how the use of your product will, directly or indirectly, improve your prospect's health. Show how your item will make him a better worker by improving his efficiency.

Virgoans are worriers. Therefore, your attitude is of utmost importance. You must be calm, forceful, confident, and sure. Do not allow even the hint of a doubt to enter your talk. The Virgo, as a rule, is doubting enough for both of you.

To Sell a Libra

These people are friendly, sociable, and harmonious. They are very interested in relationships and other people, in general. They have a strong instinctive feel for beauty and are, in fact, the artists of the zodiac.

To sell them it is important that you appeal to this artistic sense. Play down the practical mundane aspects and as much as possible leave out the petty details. Talk about the beauty of your product. Talk about its shape and form, its lines and proportions. Show the balance of its parts and the symmetry of their relations. Try to show how the ownership of this item will somehow make the customer's life more beautiful and graceful and more refined. Will your product make it easier for the customer to relate to others in any way? If so, hammer that

145

point. Tell him what other customers have said about the product.

Librans sometimes have a tendency to overvalue the opinions of others, and this may be a strong selling point. Above all, keep your presentation, light, airy, and sociable. It is a mistake to get too intense or too emotional with a Libran.

To Sell a Scorpio

These people are very intense, penetrating, and powerful. Unlike the Libra, he is naturally suspicious. Like the Virgo he is probing you very minutely, but on a much deeper level. He is not just looking at details. His keen, penetrating eye is probing your character, and evaluating your motives. His judgments are often eerily accurate.

In dealing with him keep your motives pure and aboveboard, and be brutally honest. If there are any negative aspects or weaknesses in your product or idea, spill them. Do not attempt to hide them. With Scorpios you are always better off laying your cards on the table and taking your chances; they like honesty and bluntness. In this situation you are selling yourself as much as the product.

In your presentation stick to the point and avoid all small talk. Be very serious and forceful; do not worry about coming on too strong. These people respect strength and are turned off by weakness or vacillation.

Describe your item in terms of something that will help the customer *eliminate* old ways of doing things, and how it will help him focus and concentrate on his real goals. Show him, if possible, how the product or idea can effect radical changes and transformations in his home, job, or social life. This will be sure to interest him.

To Sell a Sagittarius

The motto of this sign is "wonder and wander." These people are interested in exploring everything they see, and they see plenty. You must realize that here you are dealing with a high-level, intuitive, and extremely perceptive mentality. The mind is of a philosophic and visionary bent. If you want to interest him, you must adopt this kind of attitude so that you can stimulate that part of him. Since these people function by ideas and inspirations, do not bother stressing the mundane, nitty gritty, practical aspects of your product, nor should you bother him with petty details like costs, depreciation, tax writeoffs, or delivery dates; that is, unless he asks you. Discuss ideas, the more general and far reaching the better. Talk about philosophy, politics, religion, sports, travel, or big business. Let the conversation roam, even if it takes you into intergalactic space. You will never hold a Sagittarian's interest by sticking to one thing.

As with the Gemini stress the versatility and adaptability of your product. But do not make the mistake of adopting the cool Gemini attitude. Get excited, express enthusiastic, let yourself get carried away. Show how your product will help the customer expand on every level, materially, emotionally, and mentally. Spread before him new vistas of possibilities, new areas of exploration that can be his through the use of your product. Do not worry if you happen to exaggerate a trifle in this case. This is expected. For with these people you are not conveying dry, cold facts, you are trying to inspire and stimulate vision.

To Sell a Capricorn

These people are cool, hardworking, organized, and ultra ultraefficient. These are the executives of the zodiac. It is wise, therefore, to act accordingly. Dress conservatively, talk with restraint, and be completely businesslike. Beware of getting excited or emotional. In fact, your attitude here should be completely opposite to that of the Sagittarian. Avoid small talk and stick to the bare facts. Discuss all the financial angles and cost factors in detail. Emphasize all the practical applications and advantages you can think of. Show how your product or idea will:

1. Increase efficiency
2. Reduce costs
3. Increase productivity
4. Help the customer become a better executive

Capricorns have an innate feel and love for structure and good workmanship. If you have to make small talk, discuss this aspect. Show the quality of the workmanship, the methods of manufacture, the process involved, the amount of time, and the type of materials used, and the amount of manpower required to produce the item.

It is also wise to remember that Capricorns are extremely concerned with their careers, status, and public image, more so than any other sign. Show how your product or idea can further his ambitions and enhance his status. Tell him of other people who have used your product or idea and subsequently were promoted, or earned a raise, or made a lot of money.

To Sell An Aquarius

Here, perhaps, you are dealing with the highest mental type in the zodiac. They have original, inventive, and strong scientific minds. They are very idealistic and individualistic, and they love new things, unique approaches, and ultramodern ideas. Since the Aquarian is apt to be a bit bohemian (or at least he thinks like one), there is no need to dress too conservatively.

Your approach should be cool, detached, rational, and friendly. Adopt the attitude of a friendly acquaintance who happens to be communicating some information. Do not get too excited or emotional, and do not get too personal. The Aquarian has a wide mind so adopt a wide point of view in your talk. In other words, do not just hammer on the personal benefits of your product, discuss the benefits it can bring to many people, to groups of people, in general. Try and stimulate your customer's idealism. Try to show how the product or idea can help humanity, or if this is impossible (as it often is), show how the product can assist the person to help others.

In describing your product, focus mainly on the ideas behind it, the technology of it, the latest scientific principles on which it is based, and the scientific work of its inventor. Stress also the uniqueness of the item; enumerate the differences between it and the other items on the market. Aquarians, as a rule, like systems. If your product or idea can help him systematize his life or work, by all means tell him so.

To Sell a Pisces

Here you are dealing with the highest emotional and intuitive type in the zodiac. These people are sympathetic, understanding, and very sensitive to the needs of others, usually overly so. In dealing with him you are selling yourself. The Pisces, as a rule, is much more interested in you than in your product. Practical mundane things tend to bore him, and the average kind of sales pitch holds little interest for him.

Basically, there are two ways to sell him. You can either glamorize the product, glorify it, and stimulate his faith in it or you can evoke his wide, and very deep personal sympathies. Since many products do not lend themselves to be worshipped, the second approach is better.

Talk with feeling and emotion. Do not be afraid to get personal. Tell him of your personal problems, your personal frustrations, either in life or at your job, talk about your dreams and your deepest feelings. Has a tragedy occurred to either you or someone close to you? Tell him about it. Explain how important it is for you personally to sell these items. Describe your family and kids and explain that you are having a hard time supporting them. If you can genuinely evoke the Piscean's sympathy, nine times out of ten you will make a sale.

One final note. You should not think of the twelve selling categories as Sun Signs. You should consider them as zodiacal "types"; that is, as people who are very strong in a sign. This information is valid as a general outline. To be really exact, we would treat each prospective buyer as an individual and, of course, have his natal chart in front of us.

13

Living With the Signs

One of the central insights of astrology, which scientists have only recently discovered, is that we live in a *process* universe. Everything you can possibly think of, including the mind itself, everything you look at, including your instrument of vision, your eyes, in fact any object, person, or situation which you can perceive with your senses, and including your senses, is changing continually. As the great Greek philosopher Heraclitus said, "It is impossible to step in the same river twice."

This insight has tremendous implications in the way we live our lives and in our ability to be happy. For the unfortunate fact is that although we live in a changing universe, we think and react with static ideas and concepts. We do not see that our ideas, our deepest convictions, and beliefs, which may have been true and valid at one time for one situation, are not valid for other times and other situations. We do not see that ideas, concepts, and beliefs being made up of mental matter, are also in process. They are also going through repetitive cycles of birth, growth, decay, and death. For one reason or other, most of us have not learned to make our thinking and emotional responses *match* what is really happening in the environment. This leads to all kinds of problems, especially in the domestic sphere of life.

Most marriages or living-together situations fail because one or both of the parties are not seeing the other person's viewpoint or the relationship itself in true perspective. Relationships, like everything else in the universe, are cosmic processes and obey cosmic laws. In any relationship it is vital to know what stage or phase the relationship is in. There are only three possibilities. The relationship is birthing, growing, or dying. Each of these stages has different laws.

When a relationship is being born—this is usually the courtship or romantic phase—it is quite natural and normal for both parties to veil each other in a romantic haze of idealistic illusion. This is part of the charm of courtship. Each party sees only the good in the other, and the negatives are swept under the rug of the subconsciousness.

But when the birthing stage is over and the couple decide to enter the growth stage; that is, they decide either to marry or to live together, new factors and new laws enter the picture. The mere decision to live together and build one aura has changed forever the nature of their relationship. Neither party can afford to cling to any delusions about the other person or about himself any longer.

This phase of the relationship requires that each take a good long, sober look at the other, and see him/her as he/she/ really is. No one is perfect. We all have flaws and personality quirks. Now is the time to look at them. Now is the time to examine those unpleasant negative facts and put them against the positive to see what adjustments and changes in habits and life styles will become necessary to handle this relationship. Are we perhaps clinging to expectations, hopes, and concepts about the other which he/she cannot possibly live up to?

Are we clinging to a hope of changing the other party into what we think is the right pattern, but which in reality is alien to that person's psychological needs and structure? All these things have to be considered and weighed.

At this stage of the relationship a good knowledge of astrology can be of tremendous assistance. It is wise to have a synastry (comparison) chart done on both persons by a competent professional astrologer. In this procedure the astrologer will first do your chart and point out your own strengths, weaknesses, and needs; then he will do your mate's chart, and point out his/her strengths, weaknesses, and needs; and finally he will combine the two into one chart and examine exactly where different needs, quirks, and habit patterns are likely to conflict and cause problems. Once these are brought to light, the two parties can consciously work at making the adjustments and compromises needed to build a healthy relationship.

Of course, this comparison chart is only useful if both parties are mature and really want to make the relationship work. When this is not the case, no amount of knowledge is going to help. Both parties will have to walk through a bath of emotional-mental fire, of destroyed dreams, shattered hopes, bitterness, and vindictiveness. And this, too, is perhaps good. This, too, seems to be part of a cosmic process at work. For problems will always lead the way to solving the problem.

But assuming that most of us want to avoid problems, what insights can a person's Sun Sign give in the domestic sphere? What kind of behavior and attitudes can we more or less expect from each of the Sun Signs? Let us find out.

Aries

As mentioned many times, the central psychological need of the Aries is the freedom to act independently. You must thoroughly understand this if you are ever going to understand your Aries mate. Do not expect him or her to lead a quiet, peaceful life. Do not expect him or her to be a homebody. This is not the Arian's style.

If you try to limit the Arian's freedom of action in too serious a way, you will have a terrific explosion on your hands that you will remember for a long time. The best solution (if you have the energy and stamina) is to go out there and join him/her in whatever the person is doing.

By nature and temperament the Aries is not a liar. In fact, the reverse is true. They are honest to the point of seeming brutally frank. If you are a sensitive type, it is something you will have to learn to live with.

Do not be surprised if you find that your Aries mate is always rushing. It seems that no matter what they do, they must do it quickly. They are by nature very impatient and this can frazzle the nerves, especially when they try to make you work at their pace.

When two people live together, it means that each has lessons to teach the other. You can help the Aries modify some of these traits, but do not try to eliminate them completely. The Aries may seem selfish to you, but you must realize that he or she is not doing this consciously or maliciously. They get very wrapped up in their own thoughts, opinions, and desires and have a lot of difficulty seeing the other person's point of view. By temperament they have a "me-first" attitude.

Taurus

Taureans are noted for a calm, placid, disposition, a love for the home and material security.

In the domestic sphere this will manifest in a variety of ways. Their need for stability and calm makes them very patient and forebearing people. They are difficult to make angry, and they place a high value on domestic harmony. When they do get angry, however, look out.

Since Taureans are rather set in their ways, you may find yourself forced to live by an almost mechanical and rigid routine, which not too many people enjoy. If eating and cooking fine foods does not rate highly with you, there may be some conflict with your Taurean mate. Food, sex, and comfortable creature comforts form the center of the Taurean's life style.

Taureans are possessive by nature, and although this attitude is o.k. for material possessions, it can be most destructive when applied to humans, especially if you happen to be the object of it. They have to learn that they can not treat people as "things" to be manipulated and possessed.

Gemini

The Gemini is noted for its adaptability to people and circumstances, its ability to do many things well, and its fluency in thought and speech. If you are living with a Gemini and wish to satisfy his/her deepest needs, which is the only way to really assure domestic tranquillity, you must make sure that you can stimulate your spouse mentally. Become a good listener by all means, but also try to feed him or her with new ideas of your own. Sometimes, however, the Gemini talks too much and completely forgets about the other person. This is irritating to most people, but most especially if they belong to certain Sun Sign types—Aries, Scorpio, and Pisces to name a few.

If gossip irritates you, there may be much conflict in your household. Being by nature highly strung people, the Gemini are particularly vulnerable to fits of nerves. They get irritated and angry over trifles. They jump and fidget around with their bodies and have difficulty in staying in any one place for very long.

If they are negative types, they are prone to lying and deception. They tend to handle requests made them by debate and argument, even though eventually they give in.

Cancer

If you are going to have any kind of successful long-term relationship with a Cancerian person, you will have to become a master at handling moods and emotions. You must learn to recognize them, gauge the length of their cycles, and discover what makes them stronger or weaker. You must, in short, become sensitive to and conscious of the nature of the *feeling* aspect of human nature. If you do not, you will face a lot of conflict.

You will not understand why your Cancerian mate gets so upset by a tone in your voice, or by some remark that you meant either jokingly or innocently. You will not understand the depth of the Cancerian's reaction when anything occurs that endangers either the home or the children, even in the smallest and most trifling way. A Cancerian woman may treat a nosebleed as a catastrophe.

If you are a freedom-loving person by nature, the Cancerian's devotion to the home may irritate you. But do not try to change them too quickly because you are fighting a person who is tuned in to one of the deepest instincts of the race, nesting—a home and roots. The Cancer must learn that other things exist besides the home and children, but do not expect them to learn it quickly or easily.

Leo

The Leo is proud, passionate, and powerful. In a domestic situation, or in any situation for that matter, they feel as if everything revolves around them: their needs, their desires, their urges, and their impulses. This can be difficult to deal with on an everyday basis. Leo must learn to see and to handle the needs of the other partner, too. We can not say that Leos do not take care of the other person since they are generous to the point of extravagance, but they have difficulty *seeing situations* from another's point of view. You must make Leo aware of this.

You must also remember that the Leo feels that he or she is born to lead. With training and knowledge, the Leo is a capable leader. But quite often when they are undeveloped, this urge to lead becomes arrogance and just plain domination and bullying.

Although Leos love a fine home and just adore children, they are not homebodies. Give in to your Leo mate's need to be taken out to fine (perhaps flamboyant) restaurants, theatres, and night spots. Try to encourage your Leo mate to take up enjoyable and creative hobbies. This is important, for if they do not have this outlet for their considerable energies, do not be surprised if the Leo finds it in some clandestine affair or affairs with other men/women. This is more true for Leo than for any other sign.

Virgo

In Virgo people the critical and analytical faculties of the mind are very developed. This quality has positives and negatives. The Virgo is logical in dealing with problems and disputes. They understand a reasoned presentation of facts. If you are a sensitive type, you are likely to feel very deeply the brunt of this logic and it will probably hurt.

The Virgo does not mean to hurt you when he criticizes you or analyzes to the finest detail every aspect of your behavior. He/she is just being normal. You must realize that the Virgo cannot tolerate sloppiness in any way, shape, or form. Details are all-important to them, though they may seem petty to you. Here is an area in which compromise will definitely be needed.

Virgos are finicky eaters. They are very careful in their diets and in all matters that concern health. This, too, is an area you will have to understand and cope with. Plan your meals with the laws of nutrition in mind.

On the other hand, the Virgo person is very devoted and loyal. The men are good providers and the women excellent homemakers. They are practical and will very often put your interest and happiness above their own.

Libra

To satisfy the Libran's deeper urges in domestic life, you must provide them with constant romance, beauty, art, and social contact. They have high ideals about how a relationship should work, and will do their utmost, even to the point of sacrifice, to see that your needs are taken care of.

Romance is at the center of a Libra's existence. This can be both good and bad in a domestic relationship. The good part is that this adds much beauty and charm to a relationship. Little tokens of love, gifts given at odd occasions, flowers, and the like will probably be exchanged regularly. But in handling all the nitty-gritty details of daily life, it is not always easy to be romantic. It is often hard for a Libra to see romance in washing the dishes, or changing the diapers, or paying the bills. Thus the very desire for romance causes much disillusionment to the

Libra unless they learn that all these "unromantic," "unrefined" functions, when seen in the context of the larger picture are also romantic.

Nothing upsets a Libra more than disharmony and bad feelings. If there is something on your mind, do not hold it in and radiate ill will, spill it. Your Libran mate will understand and will do its utmost to get things back in balance.

Scorpio

Scorpios have a knack for uncovering secrets. It is really an inborn feel for what is true or false. Never lie to your Scorpio mate because you will be found out immediately. To break the faith with a Scorpio is a serious matter. They are loyal and honest people once they have committed themselves to something or someone.

You may be irked to find that your life style is too intense and too narrow in its sphere of activity. Fire or Air signs may find this particularly galling. Here is an area in which compromise will be essential. Though Scorpio derives much of its power to do from this ability to focus intensely on its most essential needs, it must realize that overintensity in one area or one mode of living can be extremely dull to other people.

Scorpios have to learn to change their opinions once in a while, too. When they think or feel a thing, very little short of an atomic explosion can shake them. It will be your responsibility as the Scorpio's mate to get him/her to take a lighter and less serious attitude to things. More humor and less sobriety will help the relationship considerably.

Sagittarius

Though your courtship with the Sagittarian was mostly fun and games, if this attitude stays during the domestic phase, difficulties could arise. Many practical problems are likely to crop up. Details necessary for everyday functioning are likely to be ignored. But life will never be dull.

The Sagittarian is not a "stay-at-home," so do not be surprised if he or she is rarely around. The best way for you to handle this is to get some of their "wanderlust" in your own bones and join them. Do not try to keep too tight a rein on the Sagittarian because their freedom-loving spirits will rebel.

They are among the most optimistic of people. No matter how rough things get they will always have some encouraging thought or word ready. On the other hand, this can be negative, too. For sometimes their optimism causes them to overlook certain precautions in normal everyday functions.

They lack a sense of time; that is, they are usually late for appointments. Plan on this when you expect him/her home for dinner or any other reason. Their perpetual lateness is also an outgrowth of their optimism. No matter how late they leave for an appointment, they feel that somehow or other they will get there on time.

In spite of this habit, your Sagittarian mate will keep life lively with wild displays of generosity toward you both materially and emotionally. A domestic spat is likely to be buried with a wildly extravagant gift that he or she cannot really afford, but which is given so enthusiastically and warmly that all emnity just melts away.

Capricorn

The positive Capricorn will seem to be a cool and unromantic person, at first. But as you develop the relationship, you will find buried a very warm-hearted and kind person. They do not go in much for talking, but they are good listeners. The men are good providers and the women excellent homemakers. These people are the most efficient and organized of anyone in the zodiac.

To the positive Capricorn, career, and professional and social status are very important and take precedence over domestic bliss. Capricorns find escape from domestic disharmony in work. However, the positive type does realize its obligations in the home. Their sense of duty and responsibility, of "doing what is right," is highly developed.

If the Capricorn is undeveloped, or negative, it will be cold, dictatorial, and very repressed emotionally. They will have difficulty expressing their feelings and will tend to solve, or try to solve, domestic spats from a sense of expediency rather than emotion.

Most Capricorns tend to push themselves too hard. Their drive for success is strong. Sometimes, however, they forget and start pushing others around as hard as they push themselves, and this can cause conflict.

Your Capricorn mate will tend to take a pessimistic view of things and it has to learn that both optimism and pessimism are delusory. One has to see things as they are.

Aquarius

Your Aquarian mate is apt to be as unconventional in the home as it is in other areas in life. If you do not have a little of the bohemian in you, there may be some discomfort. Remember, your Aquarian mate has a need to feel that it is expressing its own uniqueness and individuality.

Aquarians are by nature cool and logical people. Deal with them in that way. If you are an emotional type, you are likely to feel uncomfortable by what you consider to be their lack of feeling. You may get upset by their normally cool and detached attitude to you and to the various situations that crop up. This is their way. They do have to learn though, that sometimes it is necessary to get off of one's mental, high horse and *feel* with another person instead of merely trying to understand them mentally. Certain areas of life cannot be approached by logic, concepts, and theories, which the normal Aquarian is so full of.

Pisces

If you live with a Pisces, you can best help your mate and yourself by developing a strong practical sense of reality. Your mate is most likely to be a dreamer and fantasizer. If it is a positive Pisces, it is very likely to make these dreams come true, no matter how fantastic they seem to you. You will find them hard at work, trying to materialize these visions. But if your Pisces mate is a negative type, it will tend to live totally in its fantasies and seem to just float through life. This can be very exasperating when practical things have to be taken care of.

Your Pisces mate is very psychic and has the most developed intuition of any sign in the zodiac. If you are in a bad mood, the Pisces will reflect that mood instantly, and the same is true for your good moods. It is wise, therefore, to make sure that your own head and emotions are together during your relationship.

Your Pisces mate is ultramoody. A remark made one day will elicit gales of laughter. The same remark made a week later may call down a heap of abuse on your unsuspecting head.

You will, no doubt, have a lot of difficulty understanding your Pisces mate who will always be a mysterious quantity to you. This is natural, for the Pisces has trouble understanding itself. If it makes you feel any better, the reason for all the mystery is the Piscean's incredible changeability and sensitivity to environmental influences. It can act like ten different people in the space of an hour, all depending on what it has been doing, or whom it is with. For this and other reasons the Pisces is called the "chameleon" of the zodiac.

Your Pisces mate is not an especially ambitious mate. Although it may have to get a little of that quality in its blood to make out in the world. But in living with the Pisces, you will partake in an inner life rich in imagination, romance, sincere, and intense feeling, and sharing of energies rarely found in life except in fairy tales.

As mentioned, nothing replaces a good chart for understanding yourself and your spouse. The Sun Sign by itself gives only the general tendencies of behavior, and these are often modified by other factors in a chart. But if you can even learn to accept some of the basic quirks of your mate, which before now you thought were mental or emotional aberrations, if you can see that your mate is the way he or she is because of the astrological structure, you will save yourself much heartache and aggravation.

We cannot always change other people. Very often we should not. But we can always search for understanding and meaning which will enrich life and is the basic reason for learning astrology.

PART III

Introduction

In Parts I and II, I mostly presented pure Sun Sign astrology. In Part III, I intend to go a little deeper into the subject and show you some practical techniques and insights that are available with only a little more knowledge. If you have a basic understanding of the planets, the elements, and the qualities, then you have the necessary tool for doing some simple do-it-yourself astrology that can be quite useful and entertaining. You will amaze yourself and your friends with the insights you will get by applying these basic astrological principles.

To carry out these techniques, you will need an ephemeris. There are various kinds and styles, but for this particular work, we recommend the *Rosicrucian Ephemeris* because it is easy to read.* For those of you

---

* If unavailable at your local bookstore, write to Destiny Books, 377 Park Avenue South, N.Y., N.Y. 10016, and they will let you know where you can buy one.

who already have your astrological chart, you can interpret the planetary symbols and astrological signs using the lists in Tables 1 and Table 2.

<table>
<tr><td colspan="2">TABLE 1.
THE SYMBOLS
FOR THE SIGNS</td><td colspan="2">TABLE 2.
THE SYMBOLS
FOR THE PLANETS</td></tr>
</table>

Symbol	Sign	Symbol	Planet
♈	ARIES	☉	SUN
♉	TAURUS	☽	MOON
♊	GEMINI	☿	MERCURY
♋	CANCER	♀	VENUS
♌	LEO	♂	MARS
♍	VIRGO	♃	JUPITER
♎	LIBRA	♄	SATURN
♏	SCORPIO	♅	URANUS
♐	SAGITTARIUS	♆	NEPTUNE
♑	CAPRICORN	P	PLUTO
♒	AQUARIUS		
♓	PISCES		

If you are looking up the planetary positions for a person born in 1964, for example, you would get the ephemeris for the years 1960 to 1969. Turn to the page containing the beginning of the year of your birth, and then go through the pages until you find the month you want. The dates of the month, from the first to the last day of the month are in the vertical, left-hand column; and the planetary symbols are listed at the top, horizontally, from left to right. (Look only at pages bearing inscription "Longitude of the Planets.") To find your birthdate, put a straight edge across the date running from left to right where the top horizontal column (the planetary symbols) intersects your date to find the position listing degree, minute, and second of the planet whose symbol is directly above. It is not necessary to use these computations for our purposes, they are used for more precision calculations. For our purposes, all you need to know is in which sign each particular planet rests. Make a list containing the position of each of the planets in each sign. For example, if the date you are seeking is February 8, 1964, you find the particular page in the ephemeris corresponding to that date. Here is what the part of a page in the ephemeris for that date looks like:

Calculated for Mean Noon at Greenwich
February, 1964
New Moon, February 13, 1964, 1:02 P.M. in ≈ 23° 42′
Longitude of the Planets

Day	☉ ≈		♀ ♓		☿ ♑		☽ ♍		♄ ≈		♃ ♈		♂ ≈		♅ ♍		♆ ♏		P ♍	
	°	′	°	′	°	′	°	′	°	′	°	′	°	′	°	′	°	′	°	′
S 1	11	40	18	44	17	40	26	00	23	58	14	51	15	10	9r08		17	50	13r38	
S 2	12	41	19	57	18	53	8≈47		24	06	15	01	15	57	9	06	17	50	13	37
M 3	13	42	21	10	20	06	21	14	24	13	15	11	16	44	9	04	17	51	13	36
T 4	14	42	22	23	21	19	3♏25		24	20	15	21	17	31	9	02	17	51	13	35
W 5	15	43	23	33	22	37	15	23	24	28	15	31	18	20	9	00	17	52	13	34
T 6	16	44	24	45	23	58	27	15	24	35	15	42	19	07	8	58	17	52	13	33
F 7	17	45	25	57	25	19	9♐04		24	42	15	54	19	54	8	56	17	53	13	32
S 8	18	45	27	09	26	40	20	56	24	49	16	05	20	41	8	54	17	53	13	31

For February 8, 1964, you can see that the Sun is in Aquarius (☉/≈), Venus is in Pisces (♀/♓), Mercury is in Capricorn (☿/♑), Moon is in Sagittarius (☽/♐), Saturn is in Aquarius (♄/≈), Jupiter is in Aries (♃/♈), Mars is in Aquarius (♂/≈), Uranus is in Virgo (♅/♍), Neptune is in Scorpio (♆/♏), and Pluto is in Virgo (P/♍).

The only possible difficulty that could occur would be with the Moon sign position. Because the Moon moves through a different sign every 2½ days, when the Moon is marked as being either at 0°–12°, or 18°–30° of a sign, it could very well rest, for your particular birthtime, in like Virgo (analytical, critical) than like Leo (dramatic,

169

either the sign just preceding or the sign immediately following the one specified. Therefore, if the ephemeris indicates that your Moon is placed at 24° Leo, and yet your particular habits of thinking and feeling are more like Virgo (analytical, critical) than like Leo (dramatic, expressive), most probably, you will have the Moon in Virgo. On the other hand, if the ephemeris states that your Moon is 10° Gemini, and yet your particular emotional qualities are more solid, practical, and possessive than an adaptive, curious Gemini Moon, you will most probably have your Moon in Taurus. The only way you can understand what sign your Moon is in (in these particular cases), without doing the necessary calculations, is through studying the character traits of the emotional life. This is actually an excellent way to sharpen your perceptions in understanding the separate astrological elements at work in yourself and those around you. I will now explain the way in which the Moon, and all the other planets work through the particular signs.

Planets are heavenly bodies, which in their revolutions around the Sun, occupy different positions in the sections of the heavens (signs), every day. The planets move at different rates of speed through the zodiac. The most distant planets, Uranus, Neptune, and Pluto, stay in a sign for many years, whereas the "planet" nearest the Earth, the Moon, stays in a sign for only 2½ days. The planets between these two extremes, counting from the Earth, are Mercury, Venus, Mars, Jupiter, and Saturn; and these planets move at progressively slow rates through the zodiac. The movements of planets through the different signs or sections of the zodiac wheel are called *planetary transits*.

Each planet represents a principle or a source of a specific kind of power. Each sign represents a function or mode of behavior. Thus, a planetary power will be modified in the way it is expressed by the nature of the sign of the zodiac it is in.

Let's see what kind of energy or power each planet symbolizes in a horoscope:

Sun

As mentioned in the introduction, the Sun shows a person's deeper, inner urges, ambitions, and power of will. It represents the person's ability to shape and mold the outer environment according to his inner desires. It symbolizes a person's central motivation.

Moon

The Moon shows how a person will respond to environment, the subconscious mind, the habits of thinking and feeling which he/she normally uses to respond to life.

Mercury

Mercury shows a person's ability to think, to communicate to others, and to relate to others on an intellectual level.

Venus

Venus shows how a person relates with others through the feelings; how he/she makes love; how he/she expresses the power to love which all of us have to some degree or other.

Mars

Mars shows a person's physical strength, his/her physical energy or lack of it, how he/she will use that strength to build/destroy things in the environment.

Jupiter

Jupiter shows a person's power to expand on every level of his functioning: financially, emotionally, physically, and mentally. It reveals the development of a person's abstract or impersonal mind.

Saturn

Saturn, shows a person's ability to limit and discipline himself or herself to manifest long-term goals.

Uranus

Uranus shows how a person expresses his/her originality or uniqueness. It discloses a person's ability to break with old customs, traditions, and habits that are no longer useful, and to do something new.

Neptune

Neptune shows a person's ability to see and feel higher ideals. It reveals a person's ability to envision conditions more perfect than they are now. It also discloses the nature of a person's religious instincts.

Pluto

Pluto shows a person's ability to ruthlessly eliminate those inner and outer obstacles that stand in the way of his/her goals. It also shows areas in which a person is most likely to act like a fanatic.

These descriptions represent the basic or key concept for each of the planets. The planets, however, are modified in their action by the sign they are in. So that if the Sun in the sign Taurus (This is Sun Sign astrology, and anyone born from approximately May 21–April 21, is therefore called a "Taurus," because that is the zodiacal sign the Sun is transiting for a month at that particular time of the year.), then the person's inner urges, ambitions, and will operate in a Taurean manner (steadfastly, stubbornly), whereas if he is born during the period of October 23–November 22, his urges and ambitions will manifest in an intense, penetrating manner, in other words, in a "Scorpio" manner.

Although the Sun is the most significant planet in a chart, there are nine other planets to consider. By definition, this is not in the realm of Sun Sign astrology. The nine other planets make a transit of all the signs, and are also modified greatly by the sign they are in at a person's moment of birth. Thus the energy of the planet Venus, for example, will be expressed very differently when passing through the sign Virgo than it will when passing through the sign Pisces. Next let's see how the particular planetary forces will be modified, and sometimes transformed, by the nature of the sign the planets passing through at the moment of birth.

Aries

The energies of the planets will manifest ardently, actively, and impulsively. Mars is the planet that operates most beneficially through Aries; that is, the qualities of the planet Mars and the qualities of the sign Aries are most sympathetic or resonant to each other. Mars in Aries is a very strong position for this planet.

Taurus

The energies of the planets will manifest practically, stabley, and possessively. Venus is the planet that operates most sympathetically through Taurus. Venus in Taurus is a strong position for this planet.

Gemini

The energies of the planets will manifest adaptively, communicatively, and variably. Mercury is the planet that operates most sympathetically through Gemini. Mercury in Gemini is a strong position for this planet.

Cancer

The energies of the planets will manifest sensitively, protectively, defensively. Moon is the planet that operates most sympathetically through Cancer. Moon in Cancer is a strong position for this planet.

Leo

The energies of the planets will manifest dramatically, expressively, powerfully. The Sun is the planet that operates most sympathetically through Leo. Sun in Leo is a strong position for this planet.

Virgo

The energies of the planets will manifest analytically and critically. Mercury is the planet that operates most sympathetically through Virgo. Mercury in Virgo is a strong position for this planet.

Libra

The energies of the planets will manifest harmoniously, relatedly, romantically. Venus is the planet which operates most sympathetically through Libra. Venus in Libra is a strong position for this planet.

Scorpio

The energies of the planets will manifest intensely and penetratingly. Mars and Pluto are the planets that operate most sympathetically through Scorpio. Mars or Pluto (or both) in Scorpio would be a strong position for these planets.

Sagittarius

The energies of the planets will manifest expansively and optimistically. Jupiter is the planet that operates most sympathetically through Sagittarius. Jupiter in Sagittarius is a strong position for this planet.

Capricorn

The energies of the planets will manifest prudently, cautiously, concentratedly. Saturn is the planet that operates most sympathetically through Capricorn. Saturn in Capricorn is a strong position for this planet.

Aquarius

The energies of the planets will manifest in a friendly,
impersonal way: detachedly, unconventionally, originally.
Saturn and Uranus are the planets that operate most sympathetically through Aquarius. Saturn or Uranus (or
both) in Aquarius would be a strong position for these
planets.

Pisces

The energies of the planets will manifest nebulously,
confusedly, intuitively. Jupiter and Neptune are the
planets that operate most sympathetically through Pisces.
Jupiter or Neptune (or both) in Pisces would be a strong
position for these planets.

Thus, the interaction and synthesis of each planet,
modified by the energies of the particular sign it is in,
plays an important part in understanding a person's
makeup. The insights you will gain by learning the
planets in the signs will help you understand the deeper
secrets of personality and behavior.

14

What Chart Patterns Can Tell You at a Glance

Here is an interesting way to get some fascinating insights into some of the deeper motivations of either yourself or your friends. If you are working from a chart already prepared by a professional, you have a head start. Just refer to it and the rest of the text will be easy. If you do not have a prepared chart to work from, you can prepare a makeshift one that will give you all the information you need to work with the processes I shall describe here.

Get an ephemeris. Look up the birthday of the person you want to check out. It is best to start with yourself because, generally speaking, each of us is more familiar with his own inner world than he is with that of others. Make a list of the position of each of the planets in each sign. For example, (See Introduction, Part III.) on a given day you may find that the Sun was in Aries, the Moon was in the sign of Gemini, Mercury was in Pisces, Venus was in Aries, Mars in Capricorn, Jupiter in

177

Aquarius, Saturn in Cancer, Uranus in Gemini, Neptune in Libra and Pluto in Leo. Make a list of these positions on a piece of paper.

Now take a separate piece of paper and draw a large circle (see fig. 1). Now draw a horizontal diameter, dividing the circle into two equal hemispheres (fig. 2). Now divide the circle with another diameter which bisects your original line. You will get this (fig. 3). Divide each of the four quadrants into 3 equal segments. You will have a circle with twelve equal arcs or sections (fig. 4).

This is the basic pattern for casting a horoscope. And this is the kind of figure that professional astrologers work with. Notice that we started with a blank circle, a zero a "no-thing." As we proceeded with our creative process, the circle got more and more differentiated. The no-thing became a one and then a many. It is very similar to what happens in life. We begin with nothing, blankness, and

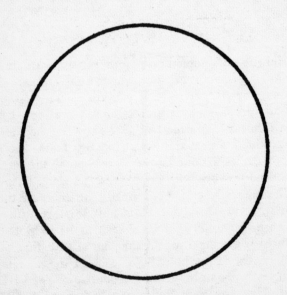

Figure 1.
Blank circle, first step in drawing chart.

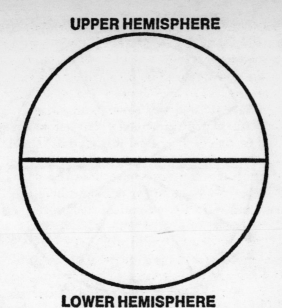

Figure 2.
Upper hemisphere: objective; lower hemisphere: subjective.

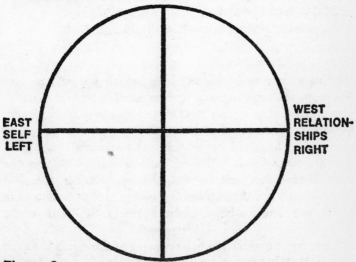

Figure 3.
The East-West axis.

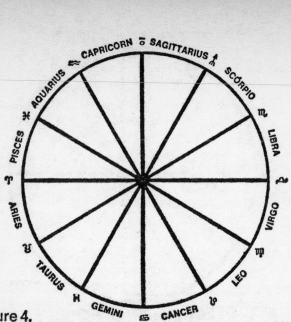

Figure 4.
Using a compass the same length as the radius
of the circle, mark off three equal sections in
each quarter; connect the marks with lines,
and you get twelve equal segments.
Now label each segment with its signs.

then as we proceed with any learning, or project, or relationship, patterns begin to appear from a general mass. A
generalized idea begins to get particularized and specific.
Order appears from chaos.

Now starting with your original horizontal line, label
that segment Aries. Working counterclockwise, label the
next Taurus, the next Gemini, the next Cancer, the next
Leo and onward throughout the twelve signs of the zodiac
until you have labeled each segment of your circle
(fig. 4).

Now make a mark in each segment of the circle for each
planet that belongs there. For example, if your list of
planets that you got from the ephemeris places two

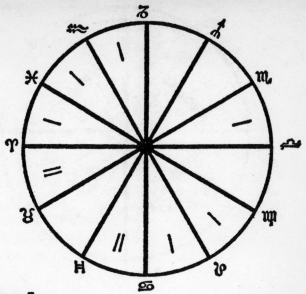

**Figure 5.
Sample chart.**

planets in Aries, make two heavy dashes in the Aries segment of your circle.

When you finish this process, you will have ten dashes in your circle. Some segments will have one or more of these dashes; some will be blank, as in Figure 5. Now look at your handiwork. Study it, with no opinions. After a while you will see a pattern in the way the dashes relate to each other and their positions in relation to the circle as a whole.

Draw a few other circles and put in the planetary patterns of other people whom you know. One circle for each person. No circle should ever contain more than ten marks. As you compare the different circles, you will notice that each circle contains a different pattern. Do not form any opinions yet, just look. You have taken the first step in astrological interpretation. You are noticing pattern. In a small way you are doing what professionals

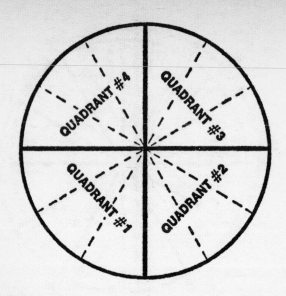

Figure 6.
The solar cross.

do in a practiced and skillful way. You are discerning a pattern of relationships. And that's what astrology—and life, too—is all about.

Take your circle and mark in heavier lines the outline of the original vertical and horizontal axis you have drawn (fig. 6). You have the form of a solar cross which is one of the most sacred symbols of antiquity. It is laden with meaning for those who want to take the time and pay the price of study and effort.

You will note that there are many ways of looking at this figure. You can look at it as a bottom and a top, a left and a right, or as four equal quadrants. We shall look at this figure in each of these ways and see what meaning we can derive from it.

Let's first look at it as four *halves* of a circle. The left hemisphere is called the *Eastern hemisphere* by astrological convention. The right hemisphere is called the *Western*

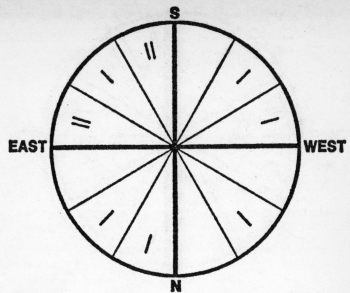

Figure 7.
Most planets in Eastern hemisphere.

hemisphere, also by convention. These two hemispheres represent the division between a person's sense of self, his/her need to assert this selfhood and the strength and power of this selfhood in everyday expression. The Western hemisphere represents a person's recognition of others, or the *not self.* It shows a person's ability to relate to others, to form partnerships with others, and to see things from another's point of view.

In life, of course, both of these aptitudes or attitudes must be balanced. To exist properly and prosper on this earth, one must be a strong and independent person, who is yet able to relate with others in a harmonious way. Both the hyperindividualism of the Eastern hemisphere and the hyperconcern for others and relationships of the West are, by themselves, unbalanced. You can see this graphically in the diagram. Both sides are needed to complete the circle and make it whole.

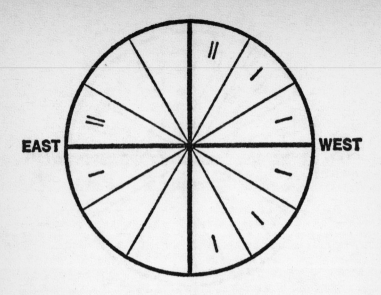

Figure 8.
Most planets in Western hemisphere.

Look at your circle. Count the planets in each of the hemisphere. Which hemisphere contains more planets? If it is the Eastern side (fig. 7), then you know that you are dealing with a very independent and self-assertive person. If the person is developed he/she will be the type that makes his/her own situations in life. If the person is negative and undeveloped, this will manifest as a selfish and bullying type person, an overly aggressive pusher, who cannot relate properly with others, a person who must always have his/her own way. Usually these people have the energy and push to keep themselves independent of most outside restraints to their desires.

If most of the planets are in the Western hemisphere (fig. 8), the person is relationship-oriented. That is, his/her whole outlook is directed toward other people; learning about them, understanding them, socializing with them, and trying to make others happy. In the positive

Figure 9.
Most planets in upper hemisphere.

type, the individuality is strong but has to learn to relate with others as his life's main lesson. He/she finds that almost every project, or personal goal, depends exclusively on how other people feel about it, not the public, in general, but one or two other people. They cannot seem to make a move without requiring the cooperation and say so of other people.

The negative type is a weak individual. The person tries to learn about himself through other people. The person sees himself almost exclusively through the eyes of other people. He is too eager to please, too appeasing in approach to life. He is constantly being forced to adapt and to live through situations not of his own making. In other words, people with most planets located in the Western half of the circle seem to have less free will than those with most of their planets in the East.

A possible explanation of why some people appear

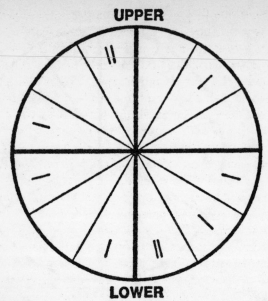

UPPER

LOWER

Figure 10.
Most planets in lower hemisphere.

more dependent on circumstance than others can be attributed to certain patterns developed in previous lives (karma), and a balancing of experience that the entity must undergo. This explanation, however, is only speculative, and is based on cause, whereas astrology deals more with practical effects, effects that you may test out for yourself.

Now let's look at the circle from the standpoint of a top and a bottom. Look at your circle and now count the number of planets in each of these hemispheres. If there are more planets in the upper hemisphere (fig. 9), it means that the person is more polarized toward the outer world, toward career, or professional and social status. If there are more planets in the bottom half of the circle (fig. 10), then the person is more interested in personal pursuits, inner goals, inner pleasures. We have all met both types of people. Some are very ambitious.

186

It seems that they have a need to prove themselves in the outer world. They are interested in the community, the city, their country, and world affairs. In the positive type, it is an urge to use their talents and skills for the benefit of everybody. In the negative type, their ambitions are purely personal. They want to exercise power and domination over others. They seek the plaudits of the crowd for their own ego satisfactions. These types will invariably have most of their planets in the upper hemisphere.

People with most of their planets in the lower hemisphere are usually the reverse. They may show an interest in career and social and professional status, but only insofar as it gives them personal satisfaction. They pursue ambition only as long as it gives them the money to pursue the pleasures that they like best. These types want inner satisfaction. These types will often decline promotions and other opportunities for advancement if these opportunities will conflict with their spare time.

Thus we have the ambitious types who derive pleasure from doing what the world wants done; and the subjective types who derive pleasure by doing what they really enjoy and the world can go to pieces as far as they are concerned.

One type has an urge to conquer the world; the other is satisfied not have the world conquer them. One is objective in outlook; the other is subjective in outlook. Understanding this about a person is very important.

To push ambition and outer values on a child with most of his planets in the bottom hemisphere is to push him against his structure. It could have very serious consequences, one of them often being a feeling of rebellion against any kind of participation with the establishment. It may force him into a deeper withdrawal from the outer world than is healthy for him.

On the other hand, those ambitious ones, who are undeveloped and untrained, have to be careful of their tendency to push their ideals and values on all of the people. They should avoid trying to save "humanity" with their own answers, until they have thoroughly tested these "answers" in their own inner lives and everyday experience.

Now let's look at your circle from a different vantage point. Notice that the solar cross gives us four quadrants or quarters. Let's label them as follows (see fig. 7):

The Aries to Cancer quadrant is #1; Cancer to Libra is quadrant #2; Libra to Capricorn is quadrant #3; and Capricorn to Aries is quadrant #4. By counting the number of planets in each quadrant, you can easily see which quadrant is strongest in a person's nature. You need not be a psychic, fortune teller, or miracle maker to do this. All you have to do is know how to count.

Most Planets in Quadrant #1

This quadrant is the most subjective, personal, self-assertive of all the quadrants. In the positive type the native is honest, independent, with a strong attitude of pleasing himself. He cares little for the approval or disapproval of other people. He will do his own thing regardless of consequences. He/she is in a developmental process of building a strong personality for service in the outer world at a later date. His focus for this lifetime, however, is inward.

The negative type is the most personal and selfish of all the quadrants. They judge all outer experience by how they see things. They judge all good and evil solely by how a thing affects their personal pleasures and appetites. If a thing gives them pleasure, it is good. If it causes them pain, it is bad; and that's all there is to it. It is almost impossible for these people to see things objectively or impersonally.

Most Planets in Quadrant #2

This quadrant is the most dependent of all the quadrants. Notice that it is located in the West and bottom half of your circle. This means that the person is subjective and relationship-oriented. They feel themselves only when they are around other people. They derive inner satisfaction mostly through association with others. They are dependent on others for their feelings of inner harmony.

In the positive type we find that there is a strong individuality, but that they are getting inner training, inner development in handling relationships with other people. Most of the relationships they form are personal, based on like and dislike. There is very little relating done on an impersonal, intellectual, or career basis.

In the negative type we find that the individuality is weak. Inner satisfaction does not come easily to these people. They find that they are dependent for their inner harmony on situations not of their own choosing. Other people have too much to say about what makes them personally happy.

Most Planets in Quadrant #3

This quadrant is a combination of the Western and upper hemispheres. Thus it is a blend of an objective and relationship orientation. This means that a person's outer ambitions are dependent on the cooperation of other people. They form relationships that help them in their careers. These are the types who feel that they need a partner in any enterprise they engage in. Their outer ambitions always seem blocked by their being forced to adapt to situations not of their own making.

In the positive type, there is acceptance of this state of affairs. They change their own inner attitudes and force themselves to adapt to and make the best of any situation they find themselves in.

The negative type, however, does not innerly accept this state of affairs. They resent that they are always being forced to adapt their attitudes, goals and plans to meet the demands of other people. They resent having to co-operate. Thus, they go through much failure and frustration and fail to learn the major lesson of their life: cooperation.

Most Planets in Quadrant #4

This quadrant is a blend of the upper and Eastern hemispheres. This makes it ambitious and independent. People with most planets in this quadrant are the most independent-minded people of all the quadrants and also the most ambitious, as a rule. They are also the most successful. Rather than needing partners and relationships to get their goals, they prefer to make things happen on their own.

The positive types are born leaders. They have learned enough about people and life and the natural laws of the universe so that they can easily get people to cooperate with them. They have a natural knack for making people see their point of view. They use their gifts to help society in a positive way. These people whether positive or negative types, generally have big, idealistic, and visionary concepts. They are independent entrepreneurs—even though you may find them working for a big concern. They will have their own little section over which they are boss.

The negative type will be very independent, too, but often a bit ruthless and overbearing in his/her ambition. They may push for positions of leadership for which they are not ready either by training or ability. They just think they are. They will couch their personal ambitions in idealistic clothing, quoting big ideas and pompous-sounding philosophies to cover their selfish greed.

Remember that these patterns indicate very important but very *general* motivations in a person's character. The rest of the chart may show many modifications, some of which may even disguise these tendencies to a degree. But if you dig deep enough into the character, you will find that these motivations are definitely there.

15

Elements and Human Behavior

You do not have to be a professional athlete to enjoy and derive benefit from active sports. And you do not have to be a professional astrologer to gain insights into human behavior from the study of certain astrological principles. There are many useful techniques that anyone can learn and apply without going through the rigorous training needed to become a professional astrologer.

Take the four elements, for example. Did you know that you can get a rather penetrating understanding of anybody just by knowing the proportion of planets in each of the elements? You do not even have to erect a natal chart. If you have one already erected, all well and good. If not, all you have to do is glance at an ephemeris and you can get all the information you need.

Don't take me wrong. This system is not going to be as accurate, detailed, or penetrating as an actual natal chart done by a pro who knows his business. Nothing can replace that. But you will get some very useful and practical information about yourself or the people with whom you are associated.

In astrology when we speak of elements, we do not mean the hundred or so *chemical* elements of the periodic table that scientists use. We are talking about four symbolic representations of the four basic constituents, or substances, or forces (call them what you will) that are inherent in all manifestation (life) on the physical or material dimension of existence. In astrology, we call them *elements*. Kabbalists call them *Chaioth Hakodesh* (the "four Holy Animals"). Hindus call them the *Tatvas*. Western science would refer to them as states or conditions of matter.

The four elements are called Fire, Earth, Air and Water. These should not be taken too literally. Earth would refer to all solids; air would refer to all gases; water to all liquids, and fire to electrical or radioactive phenomena.

As a system of classification for phenomena the ancient astrologers could not have thought of any better method, nor has anybody improved on it, to date. It makes no difference that a solid may be made of iron and another of rock; or that gas is composed of carbon atoms and another of oxygen. The important thing is the state it is in.

Anything you can think of is composed of either one or combinations of all the four elements in different proportions. Everywhere we look we are confronted with solids, liquids, gases, or electricity. Each of these substances has different properties and laws. The laws of solids are different from the laws of liquids or gases; the laws of laws of thermal radiation or electricity are different from the laws of gases or liquids, and so on. This is quite evident.

So it is with people. We, too, are composed of different proportions of these four elements. Some research shows that each one of our cells contains a point of light with a temperature estimated at 6,000 degrees. Fahrenheit. Were it not that our cells are in a lake of water, we would instantly burn up. Each cell has solid substance (Earth) and is nourished by the oxygen we breathe (Air). This, of course is the purely physiological view.

Psychologically, too, we are composed of different and differing proportions of these elements, and this proportion gives us a key to understanding our internal structures. Balzac said "Man is a dancing number." We are mathematical equations endowed with movement. And the job of the astrologer is to analyze and synthesize the various equations found in a chart to get an accurate view of the native's structure.

One of the most important equations is the proportions of planets in the various elements. The first step in setting up your equation is to count up the number of planets in each of the elements. In this context, we count the Sun and Moon as planets. Fire signs are Aries, Leo, and Sagittarius. Water signs are Cancer, Scorpio, and Pisces. Earth signs are Taurus, Virgo, and Capricorn. Air signs are Gemini, Libra, and Aquarius.

Now all you have to do is look at your chart or the ephemeris for a given date and count. What could be simpler? At the end of the process you may come up with something like this:

Fire 3
Water 3
Air 3
Earth 1

or, perhaps you got this proportion:

Fire 0
Water 5
Air 4
Earth 1

These are just examples. The possibilities are infinite. Without any knowledge of astrology or mathematics, you can look at the proportions and see certain things almost immediately. In the first case, for instance, the native is balanced and strong in all the elements except Earth. He has a shortage, a deficiency of this substance in his psyche. It is analogous to having a vitamin deficiency in your body. Certain weaknesses must manifest in the person's attitude and approach to life, unless steps are taken to correct the deficiency.

In the second instance there is an obvious shortage in Fire and Earth and an overabundance in Water and Air.

What does it mean to have a shortage of an element? To understand this we must examine the psychological characteristics of each of the elements.

Fire

Fire gives the following urges and attitudes:

1. Creative energy and power
2. Aspiration
3. Heat, passion, and enthusiasm
4. Optimism, courage, self-reliance, and independence
5. The need to express oneself in action
6. Positive, outward, extroverted behavior
7. Impulsive expansion

Air

The Air element gives the following urges, attitudes, and characteristics:

1. The ability to communicate on the verbal and mental levels
2. The ability to handle abstract ideas
3. The ability to make plans
4. The need for mental interests
5. A need to talk and think

6. Social popularity
7. An urge to be cool and detached and to take an objective view of things

Earth

The Earth element gives the following urges, attitudes and characteristics:

1. The need to feel materially and financially secure
2. Ability to handle the practical affairs of living
3. A cool, cautious nature
4. Patience and the ability to work long and hard for what one wants
5. A practical and concrete outlook on life
6. Great abilities with the hands, such as sculpting, carpentry, ceramics, and mechanical ability
7. Executive ability

Water

The Water element gives the following urges, attitudes and characteristics:

1. The need to exercise one's sympathies
2. Great sensitivity not only to one's own feelings but also to the feelings of others
3. Moody
4. Great powers of imagination
5. A tendency to preoccupation with the past, nostalgia
6. Generally, introverted by nature
7. Great depth of personality (You must really probe beneath the surface to understand these types. What you see is generally not what it is.)

When a person is strong in an element, it shows that the characteristics of that element are strong in his or her personality. When there is a shortage, a lack of the abilities and properties in the native's personality, usually causes a weakness.

A shortage of Fire means that the native does not have sufficient passion, self-motivation, go-power, and sheer raw force to attain his goals. He may have a brilliant mind and incredible natural gifts, but he or she will lack the power to push these to fruition. This kind of a person will have to learn to conserve every ounce of his or her energy and channel it to specific goals. There is not much extra to spare. They must learn to motivate themselves, rather than wait to be motivated from the outside as is usually the case.

A shortage of Air means that the person has difficulty communicating with others. This does not mean any kind of mental deficiency, but rather a communication deficiency. Very often, we come across people with brilliant minds who can not express what they mean so that others can understand. They either speak too high above, or too far below, the other person's level of awareness and understanding. When there is a shortage of Air, the native either is always misunderstood by others or is himself always misunderstanding other people. Generally, unless there are other factors in the chart that compensate, the person is usually not too interested in abstract ideas, or reading, or other mental interests. There is also a serious weakness in their ability to make plans. This latter inability is a serious weakness in attaining one's goals.

A shortage of Earth means that the person is weak in practical matters. There are difficulties in making money and especially in saving it. They are always making impractical business decisions which they always regret later on. They lack the feel for handling and maintaining material things. They have difficulty taking their ideas and making them practical and workable so that these

197

ideas can become manifest in reality. Generally, they are what we call in slang "spaced-out," "off the Earth."

A shortage of Water means that the person is not sufficiently sensitive to the feelings and emotions of other people or himself or herself. They are not tuned in to it. They may glibly and superficially be able to talk about it, but they lack empathy. Generally, their life is full of frustration because they have unwittingly hurt someone's feelings without knowing it. This is not to say that these people are consciously cruel. This is not true. They just do not realize and understand other people's sensitivities. And then there is another problem caused by a lack of Water. This one is perhaps more serious for the native's health and well-being. These types tend to repress their emotions, to hold them back, locked inside. Generally, what happens is they hold back and hold back, until they explode. That is, they unloose a barrage of emotion over some inconsequential happening, totally out of proportion to the event. Or, they repress the emotions to such a degree that they become tense, irritable, and often physically ill.

Now, don't take my word for all of this. Check on yourself and your friends and acquaintances, and you can easily verify what I have written here. If it checks out, you have a simple, yet useful tool for understanding others.

16

The Planets and Creativity

The problem of creative self-expression is more than a minor issue which concerns a few isolated persons. This problem is international and interdimensional in scope and affects every area of human activity. The source of all human ills seems to lie in the abuse, misuse, or nonuse of our creative energies: creative energies which all of us are endowed with to some degree or another.

Creative urges can never be extinguished. They can, however, be blocked or dammed up. Whenever this happens, the dynamic force behind the creative urge will seek a compensatory form of expression which is not natural to it. In simpler language we can say that we are all born with two psychic doors inside us. One is labeled "create," and the other is labeled "destroy." When, for whatever reason, ignorance, parental, societal or economic pressure, the "create" door is blocked or locked, the eternally flowing creative energies must go through the "destroy" door.

They have no other choice. The creative flow which stems from the cosmos as a whole MUST be expressed. If it can not express itself one way, it will express in some other. When this happens, the force reverses its polarity and turns negative. Thus, repressed love becomes hate, blocked compassion becomes destructive self pity, blocked creativity becomes dynamic destructivity, and all of these are accompanied by frustration, fear, and irritability, and all the other ills that humankind is heir to. Multiply this process by approximately three billion people, and you can see why the planet seems to be wallowing in a vast ocean of negative and destructive energy. The majority of humans have simply not learned how to handle and channel their creative energies. If this process is allowed to continue for too much longer, we stand a good chance of destroying ourselves and the planet. For, today, unlike the past, we have the tools and the weapons to do it.

According to many occult traditions, humanity was given the arts by the Higher Beings who supervise human evolution, The Elder Brothers of the race. For, without the arts (and the sciences which make all art possible), we would be little better than the beasts in the field. In many of the older religions, art was not separated from religion as it is today, but was an integral part of it. All priestly and initiate training required the student to become facile in a few of the arts and crafts of the day. The student was expected to learn about the creative forces of the cosmos by learning and exploring the creative forces within himself.

To learn the mysteries of superphysical creation, he first learned how to become a creator in his own right and in his own small way. After a while he came to see that the laws that go into painting a picture, composing a song, or writing a poem were the same laws that went into creating a galaxy or a universe. Thus, to him the cosmic process became a living reality in his consciousness—a dynamic life fact, rather than just abstract theory or nebulous revelation. As the semanticists would say, the student had established "referents" in his consciousness as the result of creative experiences, and was thus prepared to understand the deeper teachings.

Creative self-expression bestows other benefits, as the ancient initiates well knew. It is perhaps the best and most practical method of training and controlling the wild, unruly passions of our lower nature. It is an excellent tool for making these emotional beasties toe the mark and do our bidding. In ancient times humanity was almost completely dominated by its passions. For example, if a person felt like killing, he killed; if he saw a woman he liked, he raped her and if her mate interfered, he would kill him, too. In those days there was little check on the full expression of people's primitive passions.

Today, these passions still exist, but they are covered by a thin veneer of civilization—something like covering an active volcano with tissue paper. And although most of us can restrain ourselves from killing, looting, and raping; nevertheless, these passions periodically find expression through riots, revolutions, and wars. If humanity is to survive, it must find some healthy way to express its pent up feelings from the past which is our primitive heritage. And healthy, constructive, creative self-expression is one method for doing this.

Arts and crafts have long been a natural method for curing the mentally ill and for healing various nervous disorders. In fact, many say that the true function of art is to heal people's nerves.

No matter what we do for a living it's very important that we have a few creative outlets. But this alone isn't enough. We need outlets that are geared for and suited to our own personal and unique structures, outlets which will give us the most personal satisfaction and rejuvenation. It's not enough for a housewife to take up embroidery, for example, merely because all her friends are doing it. If she has a strong Neptune in her chart, she should be into music, poetry, or painting, no matter what everyone else is doing.

Astrology is an uncannily accurate tool for locating creative potential. Each planet symbolizes a different type of creative energy, and the signs show how these energies behave. When these two factors are synthesized properly, we come up with a portrait of the way in which a person focuses his energies. When looking for a person's creative potential, one important key we can use is the prominence of a particular planet. As each planet symbolizes a certain type and direction of force, a certain talent, we can see how finding a prominent planet would give us certain powerful indications of a person's natural bent.

In the Part III introduction, you will find listed the particular planet which operates most sympathetically through a particular sign. The planet described in each specific case is in its "home." This is where it is strongest and most comfortable. So that if, for example, we find Mercury in Gemini or Virgo, we have a strong Mercury, with all the talents and possible creative outlets that go with this strength. Also, if the Sun is in Virgo or Gemini, we have another sort of Mercury influence, because the Sun, a person's most important planet, is in a sign ruled by Mercury. Likewise, with a Sun in Taurus, we have a Venus-ruled person, as Venus rules Taurus. So that if the planet itself is in its home, or the person's Sun is ruled by the planet specified in the following descriptions, we have what is known as a strong or prominent planet. This means that all the possible talents the planet can manifest are emphasized, and one would do well to study these inclinations, as they are a "natural" for the native, and an area in which he could undoubtedly excel.

Now let's look at how the planets affect human creativity.

Sun

A strong Sun (Note: a planet can be "strong" by sign, by aspect or as ruler of the chart.) indicates a powerful and creative person who is strongly motivated to self-expression. He generally has an overabundance of life-force and vitality, and this makes the person a natural leader. This type of person needs creative outlets as a baby needs milk, otherwise, he can degenerate to using his powers to dominate others, to speculate recklessly, and to arrogant show-offness. The best type of creative outlets for this type of person is the kind that places him or her in the center stage where others can admire them. Acting, directing, dancing, or playing a musical instrument are perfect. The strong Sun person needs to be appreciated and honored for his/her creative efforts.

Moon

The Moon represents a person's subconscious mind, the habit mind. As you know it is the subconscious that supplies the raw material for all creativity. The memories of past experiences, past impressions, and emotional upheavals are all recorded in the subconscious, and these memories are the substance that is used in all creative efforts. No one can be a really good artist, no matter what their latent potential is, if they do not have any raw life experience. Their subconscious storehouse is empty, and they need to fill it before they can really do any serious work. A strong Moon person will have great sensitivity and a sense of rhythm. The imagination is also very strong; and if the rest of the chart is conducive, they can apply these to almost any kind of art or craft. Basically, though, they need outlets in which they can express their feelings.

Mercury

A person with a strong Mercury is very creative and facile in the fields of communication. They make excellent writers, teachers, public speakers, stage comedians, and impressionists. They need outlets in which they can talk, express ideas, and use their minds. They also need a lot of mental stimulation from without. They need to read and study and take courses. This is basic to their mental health and sanity. It is very unwise for a Mercurean temperament to allow anyone or anything to interfere with their mental development.

Venus

The planet Venus gives the person an understanding of, and feel for, beauty, art, and harmony. It is one thing to create and to express oneself, but to express oneself beautifully is the hallmark of the artist. And Venusians are artists to the very depths of their beings. A strong Venus bestows a natural knack for harmonizing colors and shapes, and this gives the person abilities in the areas of painting, fashion design, interior decorating, cosmetology, and so on. If there are aspects to Neptune, there will be excellent musical ability. If there are aspects to Mercury, there will be strong literary talent. But there will always be a natural esthetic appreciation and sensitivity.

Mars

A person with a strong Mars is endowed with a lot of physical energy and drive. There will also be a love of action and a need to do things. By itself, Mars is not considered an artistic planet, but it does supply the physical energy and drive so necessary for creative activity to get off the ground. It also adds power and passion to whatever one does. Thus, Mars aspecting Mercury adds power and keenness to the mind, and gives an especially strong drive for mental and verbal self-expression. Mars aspecting Venus will add power to the Venusian functions, and if used properly, will push the normally easygoing Venusian into action.

Jupiter

A person with a strong Jupiter will have a natural flair for serious writing of a long-term nature. They will also derive much satisfaction and creative release from serious studies of such topics as law, religion, metaphysics, and philosophy. They are rarely satisfied with creativity that is ephemeral and relatively unimportant. And the only way that these types can reach true inner satisfaction is through creative expression that endures.

Saturn

A person with a strong Saturn will have the discipline and the sense of form so necessary for any of the arts. When we analyze it, we find that Saturn is in reality the very backbone of all the arts and of creativity, in general. Without Saturn, which is the Lord of Manifestation, none of the arts is possible. Saturn supplies the ability to measure, to correlate, and to coordinate. Saturn gives one the ability to take an inspiration and then package it into a form. To some Saturn means the mathematical application of one's understanding and insight, and no matter what a person's creative gifts may be, if they are not applied diligently, persistently, and mathematically, they won't amount to much. Although most astrologers say that music is under the domain of Neptune, it would seem that Saturn also has a tremendous influence, here, perhaps, equal to that of Neptune, but in a different way. For the essence of music is rhythm, and rhythm means measured motion, time, which is ruled by Saturn. Saturn also rules science; and through the applied sciences the artist has the tools with which to create. Through the sciences musicians have the instruments with which to play; artists have the brushes, paints, and canvases with which to paint; writers have typewriters and pens with which to hammer or scratch out their ideas.

Uranus

A strong Uranus in a chart gives tremendous originality, force, and individuality to the native's creativity. It gives a drive to create and express all that is new, unique, and avante garde. Uranian people are extremely able and creative in the sciences and especially the fields of electronics. Besides being natural inventors and innovators, they excel in the new arts which technology has opened up; electronic music, art (painting with lights, light shows), movie making and TV. They are especially adept at manipulating the technical aspects of these mediums, which are such a big part of the total artistic effect.

Neptune

A strong Neptune endows the person with an ultra-refined sensitivity. Neptune has been called the higher octave of Venus, and there is no doubt that Neptunians possess many of the qualities of the Venusian, but with a more refined, sensitive, idealistic, and inspirational level. A positive Neptune endows the person with the vision and the inspiration which makes great art. Neptune also gives a universality and timelessness to the creative imagination. A person with a strong Neptune and who feels the uncontrolled surges of his imagination should discipline and enrich his capacities through art: as a creative artist or musician, or as an admirer of art. He or she must create and channel this powerful energy or else manifest various types of Neptunian neuroses dissatisfaction, disillusion, dissolution, dissipation, deception, confusion, escapism, or drug addiction.

Pluto

Many astrologers say that Pluto is the higher octave of Mars, and this seems to hold true in practical chart interpretation. A strong Pluto will intensify and add drive and power to a person's creative gifts. A person with a creative chart combined with a strong Pluto will have urges to drastically eliminate anything which stands in the way of their free creative self-expression. There will be a drive to create that will be almost fanatic and obsessive. When kept under control, Pluto seems to give the power to affect masses of people with one's creative efforts in whatever field.

In a natal chart many of these elements are blended. They interweave, each with the other. A person, for example, may have a strong Venus and a strong Uranus. If they aspect each other, it will show an art nature that is innovative, experimental, and individualistic. If other parts of the chart help this aspect, it can mean a genius in art. Similarly, with the other planets. The astrologer synthesizes all the factors and facts at his disposal and gets a good picture of the nature and type of a person's creative potential. And once this is done, the person can find ways to actualize this potential according to his/her structure.

17

The Practical Use of the Lunar Transits

In discussing the effects of Lunar transits, or any other planetary transit for that matter, to be really *accurate* and *thorough*, we would have to analyze the transit in relation to the person's natal and progressed chart; in relation to the environment; that is, how this transit affects the people around me and the people with whom I work and socialize? And then we would have to synthesize these two factors to find out how the transit is likely to affect the native's relation to the environment. For man is an organism-in-an environment—he cannot be separated from it.

However, there is a relatively simple technique, through which we can get a good *general* idea of the astrological "weather" that almost anyone can use in a practical way. This is watching the daily transits of the Moon. In a practical sense, watching the transits of the Moon is more useful for our daily activities than watching the transits of the Sun (though it is very important.)

The Sun, astrologically, represents a person's deeper urges—his higher self—his long-range ambitions. Its transits, therefore, set the *tone* for the whole month, and have the effect of stimulating the deeper urges in people. However, the Moon, represents the reflection principle, the subconscious mind, the everyday mind, the automatic mind that we develop to handle the environment. The Moon also rules the emotional nature of the person, and who can deny that most everyday decisions are made instinctively and emotionally, rather than through cold, hard logic. The Moon's transits, therefore, have a very powerful effect on our everyday activities. More importantly, however, its transits affect the emotions of the masses of people. The Moon rules the behaviors of the masses and its transits are a key to the fluctuating subtones of each day, the different "taste" of each day.

Anyone involved in retailing, or dealing with the general public or even anyone who drives a car, will benefit by understanding the Moon transits. It is a good guide for knowing how your customers, friends, business associates, or motorists are likely to act or react. It is very easy to check the transits of the Moon.

One of the best ways is to pick up a daily astrological calendar. This lists the position of all the planets for every day of the year. It clearly shows the position of the Sun and Moon, which are the most important in everyday functioning. The best of these is the astrological calendar put out by Circle Books. Naturally, the Moon's energy can be expressed positively or negatively, depending on how we use it.

When the Moon is in Aries

Positive: A good time to start new projects and for creativity, in general.

Negative: People will most likely to be hot-tempered, argumentative, impulsive. Accidents are likely to occur if one isn't careful. Most people's emotions will be expressed aggressively. Not a good day for making important decisions that require thought and planning. People are likely to be very self-centered and unaware of others.

When the Moon is in Taurus

Positive: A good day for enjoying domestic tranquillity, for relaxing at home with the family. A good day for doing practical things and things that require patience.

Negative: People are likely to get pushy and stubborn. Not a good day for winning someone over to your point of view.

When the Moon is in Gemini

Positive: A good day for writing, publishing, and short travel. Also for public speaking, selling, and all forms of communication.

Negative: People will be nervous, flighty, and vacillating. There's also a good chance that people will talk you to death.

When the Moon is in Cancer

Positive: A good day for domestic activities and business. The imagination will be active and can be used for all sorts of creative activity.

Negative: People will be clannish and overly sensitive. Watch your speech, there's a good chance it will be misinterpreted. People will be overly sentimental and melancholic. They may bring in an ocean of memories and emotions.

When the Moon is in Leo

Positive: Great day for making babies, both physical and mental; for enjoying yourself, for love affairs, for dancing, drama, and the theatre. Good for exercising leadership.

Negative: People are likely to be bossy and arrogant. There may be wild speculations and gambling; don't get swept up in it.

When the Moon is in Virgo

Positive: Good day for taking care of details, for systematizing yourself. Also for writing and helping others. Good day for analysis.

Negative: People will tend to get "picky" and overly critical. People will be excessively worried and tend to lack self-confidence. This may affect you and cause self-doubt and self-criticism if you go along with it.

When the Moon is in Libra

Positive: Good day for associations of all kinds, business, social, fraternal. Good day for artistic pursuits; for mediating disputes, for planning and making decisions.

Negative: People will tend to be lazy and lackadaisical, especially employees. Not a good day for housework.

When the Moon is in Scorpio

Positive: Good time to study occult subjects, to do research of any sort. This is the time to get into the "nitty-gritty" of things, for regeneration.

Negative: People's passions will be aroused. They will feel a powerful drive in them they don't understand, and it will probably be expressed through sex (of the "quickie" variety, not love), arguments, and fights. Bad day for an operation. People will be overly jealous, brooding, and morose. Don't insult anyone today, for they are likely to hold a grudge.

When the Moon is in Sagittarius

Positive: A good time for studying philosophy, religion, law, and occult subjects. A good day for travel and socializing and just being free. Also good for writing and publishing.

Negative: People will be very restless and flighty. They will be hard to pin down. There will be a lack of persistence among employees. People will be overexpanding in all areas, mentally, physically, and materially. Watch out for trigger-happy emotions among your associates. The emotions are likely to be fiery.

When the Moon is in Capricorn

Positive: This is the day to structure and order things on all levels: physical, emotional, mental, and material. Good day for organizing and getting things done; making money.

Negative: People will be depressed and melancholy. They are likely to get dogmatic, fixed, and rigid. There will be a difficulty in expressing emotions and an ultra-sensitivity. Also not a good idea to insult anyone, for grudges will be kept.

When the Moon is in Aquarius

Positive: A good time for mental and scientific pursuits, for writing and communicating, for new insights and intuitions. Excellent for associations: groups, clubs, and societies.

Negative: People will tend to get too "spaced-out," and caught up in ideas and theories that are impractical dreams. People will behave unconventionally, so don't get upset when it happens.

When the Moon is in Pisces

Positive: A good time for writing and reading poetry, for playing and listening to music, for helping others. A good time for spiritual activity, occult studies, and associations.

Negative: People will seem to be in another world; they will not be focused on the physical plane. They will be day-dreaming, fantasizing and very lackadaisical. There will be an increase in alcoholism and drug taking. People will tend to get sloppily emotional and very sensitive. Day-dreaming drivers are likely to cause accidents.

To repeat, this analysis is very general, the variations of the effect of a lunar transit are infinite. But you should take the general guidelines as you would take a weather report. It may not rain, but it is a good idea to carry an umbrella.

18

The Importance of the Qualities

Here is another easy way to get a good *general* idea of a person, *quickly*. Check to see how many planets he has in what quality or quadruplicity. By *qualities* we mean the classifications of *cardinal*, *fixed*, and *mutable*, into which the twelve signs are divided:

Cardinal: Aries, Cancer, Libra, Capricorn
Fixed: Taurus, Leo, Scorpio, Aquarius
Mutable: Gemini, Virgo, Sagittarius, Pisces

These qualities show *how* a person expresses himself outwardly, the *objective* side of the nature, the actual actions in relation to others and the outer world. In *Astrology in Modern Language,* Richard Vaughn makes an interesting statement about the ascendant, but it is applicable to the qualities, too. In effect, he says that we live in a society in which the package and the form is almost more important than the content. Most people in this culture look only at surfaces and don't bother to look underneath. Since the ascendant is the *image* we present to the public, it is a vital factor since more often than not we will be judged by our image. This applies to the qualities, too, since they indicate the person's *outer* expression, which along with the ascendant, are the most readily perceptible parts of us. Chances are we will be judged by others on this basis. How others judge us is vital in (1) our career (promotions, job, success), and (2) personal relationships; both social and domestic.

These two categories, of course, represent a good chunk of our lives (for some people it represents everything). Our success or failure in these areas will, to a large degree, determine our happiness in life.

Let's examine the qualities in detail. There are three basic modes of motion or expression in the universe. These are

1. Outward, centrifugal, initiating motion: *cardinal*
2. Inward, centripetal, passive motion: *fixed*
3. The combination of inward and outward: transitory, vibratory, flexible motion: *mutable*

In reality (and functionally), these motions or qualities are just different aspects of *one* motion. *They are a unity.* They cannot exist alone or in isolation. For example, you cannot have a forward movement in space, without automatically setting up a resistance to that movement. Likewise, "resistance to motion" implies that the resistance is overcoming some definite tendency to move.

If I lift my arm up and try to hold it steady, forces are immediately set up to try to move it. It takes a lot of energy for me to "resist" these forces (gravity, wind,) I cannot do it for too long. So it is with everything around us. Stability leads to movement, movement leads to stability. Life is a pulsation between action and rest.

215

This pulsation would correlate with the mutable quality of motion.

Therefore, all three qualities in proper proportion are necessary for healthy functioning in the real world. This is how nature works, this is how man must work to stay healthy and accomplish his goals. *The qualities are our connection to the environment,* our means of objective expression.

Cardinal

The *cardinal* person sees the environment as something to be acted on, to be changed. His law is action: ideas, theories, principles, and the like, don't really interest him. He is continually initiating processes in the environment, starting new projects, doing new things. His only interest in changing the environment is to clear away obstacles temporarily so that he can get on with his project. He will go through an obstacle rather than consciously change it. In a crisis, the *cardinal* person will instinctively *act*. He will immediately try to *do* something about it. This, of course, is good in certain situations. But sometimes the best thing to do in a crisis is *not to do,* for action may make matters worse.

At his best, the cardinal being is the man of action, the pioneer on every level, the doer of humanity. On the negative side they are restless, impatient, aggressive, and egocentric people. They start many things but never finish. Their activity seems to be for the sake of activity. It isn't correlated, coordinated, or structured, it is almost frantic. You can always tell a Cardinal person—he always looks busy.

Fixed

The *fixed* person inherently dislikes change. Change throws him off his center. Since nothing in nature is ever static, he sees the environment as something that has to be stabilized and made permanent. Whereas the cardinal person looks at the world as a place to explore—a sphere for his action, the fixed person sees it as a sea of chaos that must be molded to his will. That which he cannot stabilize and control, he ignores. One acts *in* the environment, the other acts *on* it. One is offensive, the other defensive. The cardinal person sees an obstacle as something that must be gotten through, or eliminated, and then forgotten about. The fixed person sees an obstacle as something that must either be protected against or endured. The cardinal person will go *out* and try to eliminate the obstacle, the fixed person will fortify himself against it; he will neutralize it.

The fixed people in their highest expression are builders. They consolidate the gains made by the cardinal signs and make them useful and practical. Perhaps their greatest strength is their ability to endure, to persist in their dogged way in anything they do. On the negative side, these qualities of endurance and persistence can turn into stubbornness and perverseness, a total inability to change, rigidity, and narrow-mindedness.

Mutable

The *mutable* person sees the environment as something to be *adapted* to. The arena in which he acts is himself. He will change his own patterns of behavior to meet the varying changes of his environment. He perceives the relativity of things and is concerned neither with too

217

much stability nor too much action. Flexibility and versatility are the values he prizes most.

At his highest expression, he bridges the opposites of the cardinal, fixed natures. His flexibility permits him to be either cardinal or fixed as the occasion demands. His great flexibility allows him the luxury of not going to either extreme. His cardinality is not so rash and his fixedness is not so rigid. On the negative side, his flexibility turns into vacillation, his adaptability becomes diffused, nervous energy with no direction. His is like the "Jack of all trades and master of none." He *lacks* the virtues of *both* the cardinal and fixed natures. He can't initiate, and he can't stabilize, so he winds up talking much but accomplishing little.

As mentioned, we need all three of these qualities in our nature to function properly. No one or the other is better or worse. It is the balance and proportion and integration of these qualities that is important. There are three reasons why imbalance occurs: (1) Too much of a quality; (2) Not enough of a quality; (3) Misuse of a quality.

We have already described what happens when a person has too much of a quality and that quality is overemphasized. When there's not enough *Cardinality*, the person lacks initiative; with insufficient *Fixedness*, the person lacks stability and endurance; and with not enough *Mutability*, the person lacks adaptability.

There are many persons who seem to have all the qualities in their nature, but misuse them. This usually stems from lack of knowledge and manifests as improper phasing, wrong timing. When he should be acting and initiating, he is stabilizing; when he should be flexible, he's initiating, and so on. The only cure for this is study and conscious application, especially of the laws of cycles.

Every job, project, and relationship is a cycle consisting of three phases:

1. The beginning or initiatory phase (cardinal)
2. The middle or stabilizing phase (fixed)
3. The end or transition phase (mutable)

The trick is to match the proper mode of action to the appropriate phase of the cycle. When this is done, our chances of success are infinitely greater since we are conforming to the cosmic process.

19

Future Studies

Every author hopes that he has written a book that at least a few people will understand. But underlying this is a deeper hope that a few people will be stimulated enough by the author's presentation to undertake a deeper investigation into the subject.

Any serious field of study is in reality as deep as the concentration and determination the student can bring to bear upon it.

As I mentioned many times, Sun Sign astrology is entertaining and has validity within a certain range. It is part of astrology, but by no means all of it. If you are seeking for a deeper and more penetrating understanding of yourself and those around you, if you are searching for a deeper and more meaningful pattern to live by, astrology can be of great benefit to you.

The scope of astrology is vast, and its study will lead you in many inner and outer directions. It is a philosophy, a cosmology, a system of mental training, and a science of human and cosmic behavior, all at the same time.

Here are some good texts for beginners. Charles Carter's *Principles of Astrology*, Jeff Mayo's *Teach Yourself Astrology*, Margaret Hone's *Modern Textbook of Astrology*, Volumes 1 and 2; Ellen McCaffrey's *Graphic Astrology*, *Astrology for Sceptics* by Charlotte McLeod, *Chart Your Own Horoscope* by Ursala Lewis, *The Astrologer's Handbook* by Francis Sakoian and Louis Acker, *Astrology in Modern Language* by Richard Vaughn, *Astrology: A Cosmic Science* by Isabelle Hickey.

Pursuit Of Destiny by Muriel Hasbruck and *Heaven Knows What* by Grant Lewi will be fascinating and helpful to those of you who enjoy do-it-yourself astrology techniques that allow you to do instant interpretations.

In your search for deeper knowledge of astrological principles, we recommend that you always maintain a scientific attitude. This means an open but critical mind. Do not automatically believe or automatically disbelieve anything you read. Withhold judgment until you have tested the assumptions.

As you begin this new probe into the science-art of astrology, be reminded of what the ancient Egyptian astrologers told their pupils: "Go soft, go steady, go silent, and go far."